MORE
BLOODY
WOMEN

Ireland's Most Dangerous Females

DAVID M. KIELY

Published 2009
by Poolbeg Books Ltd.
123 Grange Hill, Baldoyle,
Dublin 13, Ireland
Email: poolbeg@poolbeg.com

© David M. Kiely 2009

Copyright for typesetting, layout, design
© Poolbeg Books Ltd.

1 3 5 7 9 10 8 6 4 2

A catalogue record for this book is available from the British Library.

ISBN 978-1-84223-411-2

Typeset by Patricia Hope in Sabon 11.5/15
Printed by
Litografia Rosés, Spain

www.poolbeg.com

For McKenna, as ever

Acknowledgements

I wish to thank the many individuals and organizations that made this book possible. They come from both sides of the border, Britain and the United States. All gave their time and assistance willingly and with few reservations, enabling me to present the many – and often opposing – sides to each case I covered. My thanks go first to An Garda Síochána, whose Press Office and National Bureau of Criminal Investigation were invaluable resources. Thanks also to individual Garda officers and staff. The Police Service of Northern Ireland likewise helped enormously, and freely gave me the benefit of their experience and documentation.

Thanks to the men and women of the Central Statistics Office Ireland, who ensured that the numbers added up. Thanks to the National Archives of Ireland and to the Public Record Office of Northern Ireland.

Thanks to the families and friends of victims and perpetrators alike, who shared some of their sorrow as well as their valuable insights into the cases.

Thanks to many journalists, including Darren Boyle, John Burns, Emer Connolly, Carol Coulter, Jimmy

Cunningham, Gerard Doherty, Charlie Mallon, Deborah McAleese, Mick McCaffrey, Dearbhail McDonald, Emilu Moulton, Niamh O'Connor and Victoria O'Hara, whose work I relied on frequently.

A special word of thanks to Christina McKenna for her encouragement at each step of the way towards the book's completion.

And finally my thanks to editor Brian Langan and the rest of the team at Poolbeg Press for their unstinting support, valuable criticism and patience.

Author's Note

I have reconstructed certain scenes and conversations for the benefit of the narrative, while at the same time ensuring that such reconstruction remained faithful to the essence of the testimony given.

Contents

Introduction

Welcome to the dark world of the lethal Irishwoman.

Before continuing, allow me first of all to make one thing clear: the women of Ireland are far less inclined to kill than their menfolk, a pattern common to every nation on every continent. Women are simply less violent than men. While it's true that infanticide is traditionally associated with women – historically it was known as "concealment of a birth" – this particular crime, terrible though it is, was never regarded in the same light as the killing of an adult, or indeed an older child. In the eighteenth century, infanticide was so widespread that court sentences had to be reduced due to the sheer number of women being found guilty. Lack of effective birth control gave rise to a great many unwanted children. We are indeed fortunate that this particular form of murder has become far less common in modern Ireland – for a number of reasons, not least a growing tolerance across society in general. The familial shame attached to a daughter giving birth to an "illegitimate" child has largely disappeared; improved social services and childcare have undoubtedly saved the lives of many infants.

Poisoning too was long regarded as the *modus operandi* of the woman bent on murder. No longer. Forensic science has caught up with the poisoner – at least as far as the "classic" poisons are concerned: cyanide, arsenic, strychnine, aconite and the like. We have moved far away from Victorian times, considered to be the "golden age" of poisoners, male and female. It is still used, of course; Sharon Collins's would-be hit-man smuggled a quantity of the super-deadly ricin through airport customs. Being colourless, the lethal substance could masquerade as contact-lens cleaner.

Poisoning falls into the category of "soft killings"; suffocation is another. They differ enormously from the "brute force" style of murder, a method we associate with male killers.

Garda records for murder and manslaughter in 2003 (the most recent to show crime by gender) put the figure for that year at thirty-three, of which only one was perpetrated by a woman. Does this make Irishmen more than thirty times deadlier than Irishwomen? On the face of it, yes.

Yet we see the female killer in a light very different from her male counterpart, particularly when she kills her own offspring. Our gut feeling tells us that the "bloody woman" is an unnatural being – a monster even. But this is an emotional and not a rational perception. The female

2

killer offends in ways that touch on a part of our biology that has remained virtually unchanged down through the millennia. We are still hunter-gatherers; the male hunts and the female gathers up after him. The male carries the weapon and the female looks on as he uses it to deadly effect.

The woman who kills offends our love of order; she turns our world of perception on its head. In fact, she frightens us so much that we try to explain her killing as evidence of "evil" – the word being used as a noun, not an adjective. We see the woman as an embodiment of wickedness.

And so it is that when an Irishwoman is arraigned on a murder charge, she's scrutinized by the media far more closely than a male accused would be. As with a highly venomous but pleasingly coloured insect, her appearance is held under the microscope and studied. And invariably commented upon to an unhealthy degree.

Yet it would be churlish to accuse the media of skewing our judgement. They know what it is we wish to see most, no matter what our gender, no matter what the subject of the news story: pictures of women. A man charged with the murder of his wife or partner is seen going to and from the court dressed in a dark suit and tie – just let him appear in jeans and tee-shirt and he won't be taken seriously. His legal counsel will have impressed upon him the importance of sober and neat clothing. We study his face and shake our heads. Sometimes we'll wonder how such a "respectable looking man" could be

3

guilty of so heinous a crime. We pass on to the details of the case.

Not so with a female suspect. We are shocked by the very idea that a woman could commit such a vile act. We look for visual clues in an attempt to explain it. God help her if she's fair-haired. She's the Blonde Devil, the Blonde Butcher. If her hair is dark she's the Black Widow.

And let her dare to appear before the court in anything other than a prim outfit. A whisper of cleavage, a hemline slightly above the knee and she's a slut; expensive-looking jewellery makes her a gold-digging harlot. We study the face closely and decide she's wearing an indecent amount of make-up.

It's human nature to allow such prejudices to colour our perception, and most of us are guilty of this to a greater or lesser degree.

Inside the Irish courtroom, however, other rules apply. Or better said: there are no hard and fast rules that decide how a court will treat a woman accused of murder. Some may argue that judges are especially lenient. Others may say that men get an easier ride. The fact is that each case is decided on its own merits, and that is how it should be.

Chapter 14 examines the case of Sharon Collins, the County Clare woman who attempted to engage a hit-man to dispose of her partner and his two sons. The sentence handed down to the would-be assassin was identical to that imposed on Sharon: the judge sent both to prison for six years. Yet it was Sharon who instigated the crime – she was the "mastermind", and no murder took place. The hit-man tried to blackmail the victims instead of fulfilling Sharon's "contract".

Contrast her six-year sentence with that imposed on Patrick Gillane, a County Galway farmer who hired two men to kill his wife Philomena in 1994. Her corpse was found in the boot of a car. Seven months pregnant, she'd been stabbed six times and shot in the back. Her husband was sentenced to eight years in prison but was freed in 2003, having served only six for the vicious murder.

Research conducted in the United States points up several salient differences between men and women who kill. Women, it seems, are more inclined to kill within the home, and the victim of a female killer is likely to be intimately known to her. In other words, it rarely happens that a woman will kill a stranger; her victim will almost invariably be close to her, in both the physical and emotional sense.

Several cases in *More Bloody Women* are concerned with pleas of self-defence. The woman may have been brutalized by a violent spouse or partner over a number of years. She finally snapped on finding herself in a kill-or-be-killed situation. And yet once again we find a difference between male and female behaviour in the matter of self-defence. It appears that the woman so threatened will not respond as a man would; she will not usually kill in the heat of the moment. Rather she will plan her abuser's killing, internalizing her fury – turning her hurt and anger inwards – and awaiting an opportunity to strike. Dr Deborah

Schurman-Kauflin, author of *The New Predator: Women Who Kill* (2000), sees this internalizing as a very important factor, "as it combines with gender role expectation. Women are not supposed to be confrontational and violent. They are expected to be maternal and feminine."

Schurman-Kauflin also identifies lack of money as a trigger to murder – but not in the same sense that drives men to kill. It is important to note, she says, that

> females who kill one time [as opposed to serial killers] often suffer from lack of legal and extralegal resources due to having little money . . . It is also known that females typically kill in an abusive situation, and they kill because they lack the resources, both monetary and social, to leave . . . Lack of money affects resource availability, and as the female who kills one time is often unemployed or trapped in a menial job, with little education, she often has little money with which to retain legal counsel . . . When a female lacks resources, she can feel trapped and helpless to remove herself from the situation . . . When trapped, desperation can impact decision-making, and it is here that females are most prone to kill.

It is significant also that most women who kill are to be found among those with a very "traditional" outlook on gender roles. They'll believe that women are the "caretakers", whose duty is to marry, have children and tend to the family. The difficulties arise when those values are found to be causing unhappiness and non-fulfilment in the woman's own relationship. Because she's placed herself in a very conservative "female" role, she has no outlet for the anger she feels when things go awry. So she turns the anger inward: her self-esteem takes a pounding and she falls prey to depression.

If we look for trends in Ireland's "bloody women", it soon becomes clear that in recent years the knife – and occasionally the gun – has replaced poison and suffocation as the female weapon of choice. We have long been conditioned to accept that women are less experienced than men in the use of weapons. Yet this collection alone details no fewer than *nine* deaths from stab wounds, the victims being Tracey Butler (1993), Patrick Sammon (1997), Peter Comerford (1998), Farah Noor (2005), John Malone (2006), Emma McLoughlin (2006), little Glenn and Andrew Keegan (2006) and Jessica Prendergast (2006). It will be seen that the majority of the stabbings took place in the present decade.

This is curious. The knife is by no means a modern weapon: it's been around for longer than recorded history – as a brief browse through a museum of archaeology will show. Knives are intrinsic to every Irish kitchen and always have been. Yet the fact remains that very few Irish female killers knifed their victims prior to the 1990s. When Susan Christie slashed to death her love-rival Penny McAllister in an Antrim forest in 1991, she shocked a nation, the more because months of planning had gone into the terrible crime.

Stabbing is an unusually violent act. The force expended goes far beyond the pulling of a trigger. It could be argued that Ireland would see far more gun crime were we to follow the American model and relax the laws that restrict the ownership of handguns. It's difficult to counter this. The gun is all too often used by Americans to end domestic disputes – the killers are largely men but the women are catching up at an alarming rate. Only this year, on 14 January 2009, Barbara Sheehan was convicted of killing her spouse using not one but two handguns. The New Yorker shot her Irish-American husband, a retired policeman, who'd frequently threatened to shoot *her* – when he wasn't brutalizing her. This was a man who kept hundreds of bullets and eleven knives in his bedside locker. And this in a country with more guns in private ownership than there are people.

Stabbing is frequently the act of a demented person. There have been efforts past and present to connect such deranged behaviour with premenstrual tension. However, while it's true that PMT can and does affect a small minority of women dramatically, it's highly unlikely that it lay at the root of many fatal stabbings by Irishwomen. Personally I'm inclined to look for other motives, chief among them being provocation caused by persistent physical abuse by a spouse or partner. Nevertheless it remains a mystery why recent years have produced such a spate of stabbings.

The cases presented in the following pages – apart from two or three that also entailed the woman's suicide and those that ended in acquittal – are those in which the perpetrator was apprehended, brought to justice and sentenced. As we know, the most successful murderers are those who can kill and escape detection.

It's also true to say that statistics are notoriously difficult to evaluate. A little over a decade ago, in 1998, a survey of twenty-nine European and North American cities found that Dublin ranked among the lowest rated for murder. Fast-forward to 2007. Garda crime figures showed that Irish murders were up by thirty per cent over the previous year. There were seventy-eight in total in the Republic. Only four of those were committed by women. This suggests that in that year men were 19.5 times more likely to murder. In 2008 the numbers were higher still: that year saw a further rise of thirty-one per cent, of which several were committed by women.

It would be beyond the scope of this book to examine the reasons for this sudden escalation in murder by a female hand. Gangland killings, an all-too-common feature of Irish murder, touched not at all on the lives of the women featured here. Illegal drugs and alcohol played a part, but alcohol has featured in a great many Irish murder cases since records began.

It would seem that Irish society in general has become more violent, and that this trend is reflected in crime perpetrated by the "fairer" sex.

Another reason is that detection has become more sophisticated. Garda and the Police Service of Northern Ireland (PSNI) officers rely increasingly on DNA testing, a comparatively recent forensics tool. In short: statistically more murders are being detected and solved.

My original intention was to begin this book where its predecessor *Bloody Women* began, in Victorian times, and to chart the dark deeds of Irishwomen up to the present day. The cases were there. Every decade produced at least one murderous female: Galway nurse Mary Rielly who roasted her patient alive in 1887 (I reference the case in Chapter 17); Mary Daly, hanged alongside her lover in Tullamore Jail in 1903 for killing her husband; Agnes Black of Armagh who, with her sister-in-law's help, poisoned her aged mother in 1905; Julia O'Neill of Wexford who persuaded her lover to brutally slay a gossiping neighbour in 1926; Elizabeth Agnes Rhodes who, in 1933, bludgeoned her husband to death with a hammer and attempted to burn the corpse; Agnes McAdam of rural Galway who dispatched a hated neighbour in 1946 by having his wife feed him a strychnine-laden cake . . .

The list goes relentlessly on. Yet the murder curve suddenly soars at or close to the beginning of the 1990s – from the time in 1989 when Kathleen Bell contracted a man to murder her husband.

The Catherine Nevin case was arguably the most infamous of these recent cases. She was brought to trial in January 2000; therefore it could be said that this landmark case ushered in a new era for Ireland's "bloody women". A new millennium seemed to indicate an increase in female killers in the Emerald Isle.

It is, to be sure, a disquieting thought.

1

MAJELLA BOLAND
Murder by Proxy in Limerick

Towards the close of the 1980s Limerick had acquired an unwelcome nickname, one that did not sit at all well with its decent, law-abiding citizens: Stab City.

The Celtic Tiger was clearing its throat in readiness to roar: the country was about to take off economically; money was flooding in from overseas investment. With the wealth came a desire to celebrate. Alcohol would no longer suffice in the toasting of this new-blown prosperity. The demand for recreational drugs – cannabis, ecstasy and cocaine – would soon take hold. At the ready stood the gangs of Limerick, eager to answer the swelling clamour. There was money to be made – by the truckload.

The gangs sprang from an area in the south of the city: the less prosperous quarter that contains the old corporation estates. One such is Southill. It's made up of a number of poor streets, among them Donough O'Malley Park, which loops through much of Southill.

In February 1989, over a five-week period in Limerick City, ten people were admitted to hospital with stab wounds. In that same period, there was a riot in O'Malley Park. Two Garda officers who went to investigate several joyriding incidents were attacked. They called on reinforcements; the police found themselves baton-charging a mob of some one hundred youths. Ten of the offenders were arrested and two Gardaí ended up in hospital.

Seven years before, in 1982, RTÉ's *Today Tonight* programme invited a Belfast economist named Mary McAleese to participate as a panellist. The topic was Southill.

"There's a serious area of deprivation here," she observed. "It's a cycle of poverty and deprivation which is leading people . . . down into the criminal milieu. What I'm afraid of in an area like Southill is that we have an army of alienated children waiting for the call."

Ms McAleese would go on to become the second female President in Ireland's history; Southill would go on to become a lot worse than she predicted. At the time of writing, the area is awash with the most modern weapons. Forget knives; these days the weapon of choice is the AK47. In Southill's O'Malley Park two decades ago the most lethal weapon was a double-barrelled shotgun. On 2 March 1989 one such weapon fired at point-blank range took the life of Patrick Boland. His killer had been hired by his wife Majella. The bounty on his life was a mere IR£200.

Majella Keane met Patrick Boland in 1984. They were working at the same factory: Lyons Aluminium. She was just seventeen, having left school with an honours Intermediate Certificate. He was a year older and was employed as a fitter and electrician with the company.

It was clear from the outset that Patrick was not the finest of marriage material. Majella's mother didn't approve and urged her daughter not to get involved with him. She must have seen the early warning signs. Patrick was moody and unpredictable; worse, he was domineering by nature. But love, as so often is the case, was clouding the young girl's judgement. Perhaps she was too impatient for that white wedding dress or eager to rebel against the woman who'd always had her best interests at heart. Whatever the reason, when Majella announced that she and Patrick Boland were to be married there was nothing much Mrs Keane could do but stand back and let her daughter make her own mistakes.

The beatings began within weeks of the wedding vows being made.

Majella endured the cruelty, suffering in private. Too proud to turn to her parents for advice, too afraid to seek the help of social services and too terrified to leave the marriage, she struggled on. Not that her parents weren't aware of what was happening: they occupied the house next door. But Paul Keane, Majella's father, "preferred not to interfere". On one occasion while visiting her home, he heard a commotion from upstairs.

"You're hurting me!" Majella screeched. "You're tearing the hair out of my head."

But you don't come between husband and wife. That at least was the wisdom Mr Keane had received at an early age.

13

Nor did the Bolands' other neighbours consider it to be "their place" to interfere, despite the raised voices and pitiful screams that often woke them from their slumbers. Majella had one good friend, however: a widow, Jean Folan, who lived close by. Jean too was aware of the troubled marriage, but felt powerless to intervene. That was to change. She would come to Majella Boland's aid later on, when dealing with Patrick was on the cards.

In July 1985 Majella discovered she was pregnant. She was delighted. Perhaps a baby would change things between them and bring out the loving side in Patrick. She waited until he'd had his supper before breaking the great news.

"Pat, you'll never guess. I'm pregnant."

"What!"

"I'm seven weeks. Isn't it . . . isn't it . . . great?"

She had the words out before she realized her error. The atmosphere in the tiny kitchen had darkened. Her husband was glaring at her as though she'd spoken an obscenity. He pushed aside his plate and rose from the table.

"What the fuck are you talking about?"

Majella was backing towards the door. "You're . . . you're going be a father, Pat. I . . . I thought you'd be pleased."

In an instant he had her pinned against the wall, his hand around her throat.

"What makes you think I want to be a father?"

She could hardly breathe or speak. But Patrick wasn't seeking an answer to his question.

"Well, I've got news for you, you fucking bitch. I'm not ready to be a father at this fucking present moment in time."

With that he flexed his right knee and rammed it several times into her abdomen.

Majella collapsed, her agony almost unbearable. Patrick left the house without a backward glance. Eventually she managed to phone a doctor. But it was too late. Within hours she suffered a miscarriage.

Patrick had taught her a lesson: he was not to have his authority challenged. He would reinforce this seven months later, when Majella found herself pregnant for the second time; he reacted with the same degree of savagery and she miscarried again.

But Majella had her heart set on becoming a mother. A year later she carried a third pregnancy to term and little Leonie was born. Friends could see she dearly loved her baby and was a "very attentive" mother. But with three in the home things grew steadily worse. Patrick was clearly unhappy with the new situation.

Majella should have known that her husband would resent the baby. Immature men often do, when they feel that the newcomer has become the prime focus of attention in the home, a focus they've jealously guarded as theirs by right. It was not that Patrick had no wish to be a father; Patrick had no wish to vie with a child for the mother's care and affection.

The beatings resumed. With one difference: now the wailing of an infant reverberated through the house along with the cries and screams of the mother. It was a sorry state of affairs. But provided her abuser didn't harm the child Majella Boland was prepared to sacrifice herself, continuing to be a punch-bag and a scapegoat for his frustrations.

It could only be a matter of time, however, before things would deteriorate further and Patrick would start in on the baby. He came close enough. On one occasion he threatened to throw the little bundle down the stairs. On another he dangled her from the window of a first-floor bedroom. The thought of his injuring Leonie was too much for Majella to bear and finally she summoned the courage to leave him.

The blow to Patrick's self-esteem was incalculable. Men leave women; surely that's integral to the natural order; women do not leave their men. In Patrick's world his wife had done the unthinkable; she'd brought shame on his household. How could he show his face in public again? He'd be a laughing-stock. So he took off to England.

Mother and daughter could now live in peace. But not for long. England would prove to be a cold house for Patrick Boland. He missed his friends; he missed the craic in Limerick. To his bemusement, he'd found himself missing his little daughter as well. Leonie was now two. The spurned husband returned after a year's absence, made his peace with Majella, vowed to reform, and promised to be a proper father to his child.

The couple reached an arrangement. Majella, in no uncertain terms, told Patrick there'd be no going back to their connubial state. Instead, the father would look after the child while the mother was at the aluminium factory. The plan seemed to suit all concerned. A neighbour reported that when Majella got home from work, Patrick would have the kettle on and a fire lit. Sometimes they even had tea together. Patrick would then return to his parents' home to spend the night there.

But Majella could neither forgive nor forget the violence of the past. The hurt ran too deep. A social worker remarked: "Looking at it from the outside, it seems like the bright flame of teenage romance died rapidly quite early on."

All might have continued peacefully, though, had Patrick left well enough alone. But he had it in for Majella; if she could not forgive his abuse then he could not forgive the shame she'd caused him. Out of the blue, he made a new threat. It was one that would seal his fate. He threatened to return to England and take Leonie with him.

Majella was terrified by the very idea. He was with the child for the best part of the day. What if he made good on his threat? She wouldn't be there to protect her daughter. No, she simply could not risk it. Drastic measures were called for; it was either Leonie or her husband. The one meant the world to her.

The other was dispensable.

Patrick would have to go – and to a far colder house than was England. He would have to die; there was no other way. She would not do the job herself; no. She could

17

not and would not. It was not in Majella's nature. She would pay someone to kill him and she knew the very man to do it.

Declan Malone, a casual labourer, lived close by in Aster Court. It was an open secret in the neighbourhood that he had links to the dissident Republican group the INLA (Irish National Liberation Army) and the recently formed IPLO (Irish People's Liberation Organisation). Majella decided to approach him. If anybody could "do the job", do it properly and do it undetected, it was a paramilitary.

The INLA, formed in 1974 – and still in existence – comprised members of the Official IRA (Irish Republican Army) who'd either been forced out of that organization or no longer shared its ideology. The INLA took a more radical stance in their aim to bring about a thirty-two-county socialist republic. They gained notoriety through a number of high-profile assassinations that included the 1979 killing of Airey Neave, the British Minister and Shadow Northern Ireland Secretary. In 1997 they shot the loyalist leader Billy Wright in the high-security Maze Prison in County Antrim.

The IPLO, of which Declan Malone was a member, came into being in 1987 – two years before Majella approached him with a view to a kill. The IPLO was a splinter group of the INLA. Their main source of funding derived from drug dealing, which was beginning to take off in Limerick around this time. They were put out of action in the early 1990s by the Provisional IRA.

Declan Malone, as it turned out, was "easy to pay". There was not much riding on the head of Patrick Boland; this was not, after all, a high-profile target. He initially demanded IR£500 but later – either because this sum was difficult for Majella to raise or Malone was desperate for money himself – agreed to do it for just £200. In December 1988 Majella paid him a deposit of £120. Malone stressed he'd be doing the job on his own; were the "organization" to hear about it there'd be trouble. Freelance killings contravened their code of "ethics".

As chance would have it, Jean Foran, Majella's friend, overheard this conversation. But she believed the plan was only to "scare" Patrick and offered to help in any way she could. Malone assured her he could "handle it" on his own.

They settled on a date: the first of March. Majella would be attending a funeral and consequently would have an alibi. Patrick had enemies enough; it would appear that one or more of them had wanted him out of the way. Malone gave her a weapon for safekeeping – a double-barrelled sawn-off shotgun that could not be traced back to him. He instructed Majella to conceal it in a kitchen cupboard. Since the killer's house had a similar layout, he would find it easily.

Malone entered the Boland house on the appointed day; Majella had left the back door open for him. But there was no sign of the target. Greatly irritated, the hit-man left.

The pair convened again that evening and drew up a new plan for the following day. There'd be no slip-ups;

Majella would make sure of that. She'd have a weaker alibi this time but that couldn't be helped. She could not be placed at the scene of the crime and that was sufficient.

Next day she came home from work at her usual time of half past five. The couple had a cup of tea together. Patrick stood up to go but Majella had a favour to ask of him.

"I wonder, Patrick, would you mind keeping house for another half an hour? I want to take Leonie to the shops." She hoped she hadn't sounded nervous. Then again, she seldom sounded calm when her husband was about.

He assented and Majella left, pushing the girl in her buggy.

It was five to seven. Patrick Boland could not have known he had a mere twenty more minutes to live.

Majella, heart thumping, rushed straight to Malone's house.

"He's in."

"Right."

No further words were needed. Majella continued on her way to the shops.

Malone stole into the Boland kitchen. Sounds of a television were coming from the front room; a man cleared his throat. Patrick. The hit-man retrieved the gun from the airing cupboard and donned a balaclava.

He chambered a shell and stepped into the living-room. Patrick was on his feet at once.

But he didn't behave as Malone expected he would. He didn't cower in fright, or beg for his life. He didn't say a word.

Instead he rushed the masked assassin.

Malone fired. Patrick went down. The blast had struck him between the heart and left lung. He was already a dying man.

In the house next door Paul Keane was busy painting a skirting-board. He imagined he'd heard a door slam hard. The son-in-law in another of his foul tempers, he concluded . . .

The injured man lay moaning and thrashing about in agony, blood staining the carpet. Malone chambered a second shell. He was about to finish Patrick off.

He positioned himself over his writhing, dying victim, a boot on either side. That was a mistake.

Patrick, in his death throes, lashed out with his legs. It was unintentional, a wild action. But it threw Malone off balance. His second shot, fired at practically point-blank range, hit the floor inches from the victim's head.

Next door Paul Keane again thought he'd heard a door being slammed violently.

Malone had no more shells. Why should he? Two should have been ample. There was nothing else for it but to use the shotgun as a club, to end Patrick's struggles. Three or four vicious blows were sufficient. The victim lay still.

His mission accomplished, Malone slipped from the house, drove several miles away and disposed of the weapon. It was never recovered.

At around twenty past seven Majella returned from the shops. She wheeled the buggy with little Leonie round to the back of the house. The back door had been left open: the prearranged signal that the deed was done. She faltered. She could not bring herself to enter. Instead she went next door to her father. She told him about the open door. Perhaps there was a burglar inside . . .

Paul Keane left off his painting.

"You stay here," he instructed.

He found Patrick Boland's ruined body lying in a pool of blood on the living-room carpet. The head and chest were a mess.

Stunned and horrified, Paul backed out of the room. He rang the Gardaí.

Majella Boland was interviewed by detectives later that evening. It was all too much for her. Planning and discussing murder is one thing; being asked to identify your husband's bloodied and battered corpse is quite another. She broke down.

"Do you know of a contract that was put out on your husband's life?"

"Yes."

"Do you know one Declan Malone?"

They *knew*. Malone had been spotted leaving her home. The game was clearly up. She admitted everything.

"Yes, I pressurized him to do it," she sobbed. "I didn't think he'd be caught because of . . . because of who he was."

"Can you explain that to us, Majella?"

"Declan was in the INLA or the IPLO. I'm very sorry."

22

She looked up from her tear-soaked handkerchief, suddenly aware of the dire implications of her confession. She was going to prison. Children do not accompany their mothers to prison.

"Will my child be taken off me? Oh my God, will Leonie be taken from me?"

Later in the witness box Majella would do her utmost to undo her admission of guilt. She claimed she only wished to scare her husband. Her friend Jean Foran would support her in this. Jean testified that she'd overheard a conversation between Majella and Malone about the payment of £200 to "scare off" Patrick so that he'd return to England.

Malone was convicted on 5 December in Dublin's Central Criminal Court and jailed for life by Mr Justice John Blayney; the judge's summing up had persuaded the jury to bring in a verdict of murder. He was led from the court before the trial of Majella Boland began. He'd refused to testify against her as a witness for the prosecution. When arraigned at the same time as Malone, she'd denied the murder charge but pleaded guilty to manslaughter.

But Anthony Kennedy, counsel for the state, wasn't satisfied with this.

"Declan Malone," he told the jury, "was a contract killer hired by Mrs Boland to murder her husband. He was the hit-man but she was every bit as guilty."

Nor was it, he went on, "a crime committed on the spur of the moment. There was careful planning in all the details."

He alluded to Majella's shopping trip and a visit to a friend on the evening of the murder. She could only have been giving herself an alibi, he said, in order to place herself far from the scene of the crime. She was as much a murderer as the man who'd pulled the trigger.

"She hired and conspired and advised Malone when to do the job," he reminded the jury members. "She is as guilty of murder as if she fired the shot herself."

But Majella had not acted purely out of malice, her defence counsel Patrick MacEntee would argue. There was extreme provocation in the equation. Paul Keane was called on to take the stand. In considerable detail he recounted countless episodes of violence his daughter had been subjected to throughout her marriage. Beatings, kickings, hospitalizations. The walls in O'Malley Park were "paper thin", Keane said; he'd heard a lot more than he would have wished. He recalled Patrick Boland once threatening to throw Leonie down the stairs. A woman in the jury gasped loudly.

A social worker in the court was appalled and sickened that such brutality was allowed to go unchecked.

"With all the marriage counselling and the very many other services now available," she said, "it's difficult and very sad to imagine something of this ferocity happening in our midst – it's a real tragedy that someone, somewhere, was not able to help before it came to such a terrible and brutal end."

It was Majella's turn to give her side of the story. She

spent a good six hours in the witness box – hers was a long chronicle of abuse. Her accounts of the worst of her husband's savagery visibly moved several of the jury members. She told of the many beatings and of her two miscarriages. Yet despite all she'd suffered at Patrick's hands she confessed to being "shattered" upon returning that evening and learning of his death. Remorse was being shown. Majella had acquitted herself well.

That of course did not mean that judge and jury would move to an acquittal of their own. The prosecutor had put his case well – and summed it up with even more flair and conviction.

"We would ask you therefore to bring in a verdict of murder," he told the jury. "The undeniable fact is that Mrs Boland was part of a cool, collected, calm plan to kill her husband."

Not so, her defence counsel argued in his own summing-up. He asked them to go for the lesser verdict of manslaughter if they believed she hadn't intended for Patrick to be killed.

The plea failed. The jury took a little over an hour to find her guilty of murder. Justice Blayney refused an application to appeal the sentence.

"You have been found guilty on the count of murder," he told Majella, "and the court has no discretion as to sentence. I sentence you to penal servitude for life."

The words "penal servitude" may sound strange in our ears today, particularly to the reader in Britain and Northern Ireland, where the sentence was struck from the statute book in 1940. It would be 1997 before the Criminal Law Act would finally abolish it in the Republic.

Yet by her actions Majella Boland had set a dangerous precedent. It was the first time an Irishwoman had hired a man to shoot her husband.

It would not be the last, as several of the following cases will show. But the fee in each case would be considerably higher than a paltry IR£200.

2

DEBORAH HANNON AND SUZANNE REDDAN

Butchery of a Teenager

"It never ceases to amaze me the fact that citizens cannot go about their business in Limerick or for an evening's entertainment without someone somewhere producing a knife."

Limerick judge Tom O'Donnell in 2001

They believed it to be the savage work of men. Young men in black: two vile killers who'd slashed and battered a girl without mercy and left her to bleed to death on a Limerick pavement.

The rise in crime in the poorer areas of the city, predicted by Mary McAleese a decade earlier, had come to pass. Her "army of alienated children" had answered the call. It was 1993 and the knives were truly out.

27

Yet the scale of the stabbings had been greatly exaggerated. The previous year had seen ten fatal knife-killings in Dublin – but only one in Limerick. And so it was that when Tracey Butler, seventeen, collapsed in the hallway of a house on Ballynanty Road, news of the terrible crime sent a wave of horror across the city.

The road lies a little to the south of the notorious Moyross warren of council estates, the city's most rundown district, near the left bank of the river Shannon. Over the years Moyross has been called many things, most of them highly unflattering: "the estate from hell", "one of the most deprived places in Europe", "the pits". At the time of this book going to press, the situation there has spiralled so out of control that the area is cordoned off from neighbouring estates by high, razor-tipped walls. It's the stamping ground for several members of Limerick's notorious gangs. You venture there after dark at your peril.

Tracey Butler was on her way home on the evening of 12 July. It was eleven thirty and she'd been out with a couple of girlfriends. Home was close by – mere minutes away in fact. She did not reach it. When she cast herself on the mercy of strangers she was barely alive. She died shortly after being rushed to hospital.

What the doctors discovered were appalling injuries both in number and severity. Tracey's body displayed no fewer than forty-nine lacerations, fourteen of which had been made with a knife or knives. Her clothing was drenched with blood. She resembled something from a slasher movie.

As if that wasn't bad enough, it transpired that the girl was a slow learner. Her distraught and devastated mother, on her arrival to identify the body, told police and doctors that her daughter had the mind of a twelve- or thirteen-year-old. She'd been attending a school for special needs.

"Tracey was very innocent," she said.

A more tragic victim of senseless knife crime would have been hard to find in this, the ancient city of Sarsfield.

The hunt was on for Tracey's killers. It was thought there were two of them but no one could be certain. At that time of night there'd been few people about, and the accounts the Gardaí were collecting were sketchy at best.

Yet piece by piece the facts began to emerge. The Gardaí were half correct: the gangs of Limerick were involved, if only indirectly.

Ten days before the murder, on 2 July, a man had been viciously beaten outside his home, minutes away from the scene of Tracey's stabbing. His name was Willie Hannon. So brutal was the attack and so extensive his injuries that he died in hospital within forty-eight hours.

Willie had worked as a doorman at Termights, a nightclub attached to the Savoy complex, which relocated in 2004. It had the reputation of attracting a rough crowd, at weekends especially. In February 1993 a row broke out between members of two rival gangs wishing to gain admittance. Willie Hannon did his duty, what he was paid for: he intervened to restore order. He was a "hard man" with a reputation, a man who often boasted that "bullets won't kill me". Unfortunately for him he took sides that night – or, rather, was seen to. And he appeared to have chosen the wrong side. That is not something you do with impunity in Limerick.

The snubbed gang members resented his interference, and set out to exact a terrible revenge for the imagined slight. The rumours did the rounds, even reaching the ears of the Gardaí; they learned that a number of men were "out to get Willie Hannon".

The gang waited until 2 July. In early evening they went to Willie's home in Moyross and, in front of members of his family and several neighbours, savagely beat him. His daughter Deborah, barely eighteen – in fact not much older than Tracey – learned of the assault later that evening. The news that her father had been beaten to a bloody pulp must have been devastating to a girl so young. Such a thing can unhinge the mind.

Details are vague about that night in July when Deborah's father was assaulted. Most of the participants were drunk and memories were faulty. Later three young men would be jailed for aggravated assault. But unfortunately Tracey Butler was there at the time, and somebody misconstrued the girl's reaction to Willie's beating. They imagined Tracey was deriving pleasure from the sight of him lying broken and bleeding on the ground. Sometimes a grimace can be mistaken for a grin. That mistake would cost Tracey her life.

The Garda investigation into the stabbing on Ballynanty Road was continuing, and it was turning up some unusual facts. It emerged that Willie Hannon had had a young lover: Suzanne Reddan, twenty-six. A mother of three, she was separated from her husband. Not only that, but Willie's wife – Deborah's mother – knew of the relationship. Apparently she took it in her stride and they were "all good friends". Furthermore, Suzanne Reddan and Deborah Hannon were the very best of mates. It was an odd mix.

So it followed that each of the two young women had a personal stake in exacting vengeance: Deborah for the death of a father; Suzanne for the loss of a lover. Tracey Butler had been perceived to smile as Willie lay battered in front of the Hannon home. According to the uncompromising code of working-class Limerick, the sins of a son or daughter are the sins of the entire family. One of the Butlers had insulted the Hannons, therefore one of the Butlers would "go down". An eye for an eye. It did not seem to matter which of the Butlers was to pay. The family would be taught a gruesome lesson.

"We planned to kill one of the Butlers: Mark or Sharon or Tracey," Deborah admitted to the police. "I blamed the Butlers for killing my father. I kept thinking about my father. We planned it after the funeral."

The two friends plotted the killing as an assassination, gangland style. They put on dark clothing, including hooded jackets, to avoid ready identification. In fact they could easily have been mistaken for young men – as was the intention. Word reached them that Tracey Butler was out with friends from down the road. They discussed it over a pint or two. Would Tracey do? They decided she would. Butler blood was going to be spilled.

But possibly the strangest aspect of the whole affair was that Deborah and Tracey were best friends at one time. In fact, from kindergarten onward they seemed to be inseparable. There was an age difference of only a few months between them. They'd made their First Holy Communion together. In their teens they'd done practically everything together – including shoplifting and other minor offences for which they'd both been arrested and punished. Girls will be girls.

"They were always fighting on each other's behalf," Deborah's mother recalls. "You went for one and you'd have the other down on you."

The death of Willie Hannon, however, was to draw a line under a friendship that had already suffered a downturn. The two went from being mates to sworn enemies. It was only a matter of time before Deborah would strike. As far as she was concerned, that moment had come.

Together with Suzanne she loitered outside a pub, chatting to some youths and biding her time, allowing Tracey to say goodbye to her friends. Then the pair made their way to the Ballynanty area.

It wasn't long before Tracey appeared, heading for home. The ambushers had picked their moment well: the road was practically deserted at that late hour; the shops were shut.

"Oh, it's yous," Tracey said. "I didn't recognize yiz, so I didn't."

32

She was smirking and pulling faces. That grin of hers had already got her into big trouble. Now it was about to cost her very, very dearly.

"What the fuck are you laughing at?" Deborah demanded.

Before Tracey could reply, Deborah had grabbed her roughly and propelled her across the road – away from the shops with their security lights. Suzanne joined her friend. They hit out furiously with their fists, knocking Tracey to the ground. The victim was yelling at the top of her voice, doubtless to summon help from the residents of a row of bungalows close by. No help came.

Tracey managed to scramble to her feet and run. She'd guessed that the beating was far from over. Deborah chased after her, Suzanne on her heels.

A man appeared on the other side of the street.

"Hey, what are you fellas up to?" he called out.

Tracey's assailants ignored him. He shrugged and continued on his way, not wishing to get involved. By the poor light of the streetlamps he'd mistaken the girls in black for males; that part of the strategy was working well.

The coast being clear, the two struck again. Deborah hauled a Stanley knife from the sleeve of her jacket and thumbed out the razor-sharp blade. She slashed Tracey's face, making a deep cut. Tracey screeched.

"Bitch!" Deborah yelled in fury. "You're going down like my father did."

Tracey, clutching her bloodied face, backed away, more angry than hurt.

"Your fucking mother is next!" she spat at Deborah.

It was the wrong thing to say. Deborah lost it completely. She slashed out wildly, the knife slicing and ripping at Tracey's face and body, anywhere within reach. Suzanne joined in with a knife of her own: slashing, cutting, stabbing, cursing. The girls had transmogrified into monsters.

"It happened so fast," Deborah was to recall later. "I don't know what came over us. I really don't. We just kept stabbing."

Two knives lacerated the hapless girl again and again and again. She went down, moaning and sobbing. The pair scarpered.

"Help me!" They heard Tracey call out weakly. "Oh Jesus, help me!" They kept on running until they reached the Hannon home.

Deborah's mother heard the two come in. They were speaking urgently and nervously in the kitchen. Sensing something was amiss she went to investigate. She found the pair pulling off their jackets and jeans. There was blood on their hands, a great deal of it. She collapsed at the sight. Girls tend to be victims of assault; having so recently lost a husband to bloody retribution, Mrs Hannon could only assume her daughter and her friend had likewise come under attack from the neighbourhood's thugs.

Meanwhile back on Ballynanty Road, Tracey was by turns walking painfully, stumbling, and crawling on all fours, bleeding copiously from dozens of wounds. She could barely see: blood from her slashed forehead was seeping into her eyes. But she managed to reach a house where a light burned in the front room. She staggered to the window and rapped on the pane with all the strength she could summon up. The curtain was pulled back tentatively and a man's face showed.

"Somebody . . . help . . . me . . ." Tracey could hardly get the words out.

The front door opened. A woman looked out.

"John, you'd better come," she said. "Quick!"

"Jesus Christ Almighty!"

The strangers, horrified, helped the girl into the house. The hall light revealed her injuries with terrible clarity. The face was an obscenity of ugly gashes from which blood still pumped. If they'd ever known the girl to see, they would not have recognized her now.

She could hardly breathe. Her bloodied eyes were glazed over.

"Water!" she gasped.

They phoned an ambulance at once. But it was too late for Tracey. The daughters of Stab City were proving to be every bit as lethal as Limerick's sons.

The Gardaí had a number of leads. There'd been a "fracas" that night on one of the estates in the area, in which both males and females took part. They interviewed several of them, holding two young men over.

But soon witnesses were coming forward to say that the Guards had got the gender wrong. Two girls were involved. It was not long before Deborah and Suzanne fell under suspicion. They were questioned; they broke down, and confessed.

The case came to trial the following March in the Central Criminal Court. A nation shook its head in disbelief that two young women – one twenty-six, a mother; the other a mere eighteen years of age – could be capable of such brutality. The courtroom was filled to capacity throughout a trial that was to last several weeks. Members of at least three Limerick families were present: the Butlers, the Hannons and the Reddans. The reputations of certain family members had preceded them to Dublin and those who knew them sensed there was going to be trouble, if not in the court itself then outside.

In the course of a trial that was to present the public with a succession of ugly – and often scarcely credible – facts, a lesser though nonetheless unusual fact came to light. It was to lead to acrimony and demands for an explanation from the Justice Minister, Willie O'Dea – who, as it turned out, was not to blame. Deborah Hannon had been serving a fourteen-month sentence for larceny in Limerick Prison. Halfway through the sentence she'd been granted temporary release in order to attend the funeral of her murdered father. The release was extended on 5 July, and Deborah received a further extension. She returned to prison on 13 July – the day after she stabbed and killed

Tracey Butler – only to be granted a *third* extension until 16 July. Worse, the time spent processing her third extension was a mere five minutes.

Deborah was never the same following Tracey's death. You cannot throw away a life-long friendship so easily; it isn't easy to kill the one you once loved as a sister. But if Deborah felt remorse then Suzanne felt it even more keenly. Her mental health deteriorated so much it was touch-and-go whether she'd be fit to stand trial. At one stage her defence requested that her state of mind be taken into consideration. The judge told the jury they must take all the evidence into consideration, and decide if there was an intention to kill. He said they must treat each of the women separately.

There were those in the courtroom that day who had long before made up their own minds that the two had murdered Tracey in cold blood, having gone to some length to plan the killing. Chief among them were the remaining Butler siblings, Mark and Sharon. They were not about to let the matter rest there. Outside the court they gave vent to their rage.

"You whore, you whore, you whore!" Sharon Butler screamed at Suzanne. "Nicole's next."

Nicole is one of Suzanne Reddan's children. Seemingly the blood-feud that began with the killing of Deborah Hannon's father was to be carried over into a third generation.

"I'll cut her up!" her brother Mark shouted.

The child was only three at the time.

The judge was dismayed upon learning of the incident. He was well aware that tensions were running high in Limerick. The feud between the families had escalated viciously with Tracey's murder and he was keen to ensure it did not spiral out of control. The last thing the city needed was more innocent young blood on the streets of Ballynanty and environs.

He had an arrest warrant issued for three members of the Butler family – the Butler siblings and their aunt, Deirdre Mulqueen – to appear before him, and had them bound over to keep the peace for three years. Similarly, their nearest relatives, the Meaneys, were ordered to give a written undertaking to leave the Reddan family alone.

The trial neared its conclusion. With the evidence drawn up four-square against them, Deborah and Suzanne were duly found guilty of murder. The jury had reached a majority verdict. The two were sentenced to life imprisonment. But "life" is a pliable commodity in the case of crime and punishment – in this instance it would signify fourteen years for each of them.

Neither woman did her full time behind bars. It wasn't even close to fourteen years; it was nearer to nine.

In 2002, news leaked out that an apartment in Phibsboro, north Dublin, had a new tenant: a woman of thirty-four. The rent was some 1,000 per month and it was paid by the state. It was found that the new tenant was working as a hairdresser in a nearby salon.

The woman was Suzanne Reddan.

She was out under licence from Mountjoy Prison but effectively free to come and go as she pleased. She even had a boyfriend, and there was talk that he was about to move in with her.

Her blood-sister Deborah Hannon had fared less well. Yet that was largely her own doing. She'd likewise been allocated an apartment, close to her friend's and costing the taxpayer a similar sum. Like Suzanne, she'd initially been freed for twenty-four hours a day. But Gardaí had spotted her one night drinking with a known criminal and her hours of freedom had been curtailed. Now her nights were spent in her cell.

It was, for most people, a strange kind of justice that was being dispensed. The revelations in the media caused more than a stir. Understandably, the mother of the victim was furious that so much leniency and "understanding" was shown towards Tracey's killers. By that time the Butlers had left the deprivation of the Limerick estates behind them and had made a new start in Manchester.

"I'm heartbroken to the depths of my soul," she sobbed, "to hear my daughter's killers are out. My little girl lies in a cold grave and her murderers are free to live their lives.

"I'm tormented by the death of my daughter," she continued. "I am dead for the last nine years and now I hear that justice has not been done. I want Tracey's killers locked up and the key thrown away! I've written countless letters to the Department of Justice asking that they be kept in prison."

Suzanne was thirty-four in 2002 when it was decided to release the pair. Deborah was twenty-six.

Young Tracey Butler, on the other hand, will for ever be seventeen.

3

CATHERINE NEVIN
The Woman we Loved to Hate

"Everyone agreed that Catherine Nevin was a bit crazy and certainly dangerous, though not a physical threat. Money and power both have a corruptive influence, and nobody doubted that she pursued both with equal vigour, but it would appear that they all underestimated her. When, over a three-year period, she solicited three men to kill her husband, Tom, she had to be taken seriously."

From Gerard Doherty's *Will You Murder My Husband?:*
Catherine Nevin and the IRA

There were those who sought significance in the fact that Ireland's first great trial of the new millennium was that of a woman. It was not only unusual; it was spectacular

41

too. It had all the ingredients a tabloid editor could hope for: greed, sleaze, passion, a hired killer.

Even IRA men lurking in the shadows.

The Catherine Nevin story had so many twists and turns, and so many subplots, that the books it spawned could hardly contain it in its entirety. Best then, within the limited context of *More Bloody Women*, to examine the story in the sequence in which the events occurred. And to begin at the beginning.

She was born in Nurney, County Kildare, as the eldest of three children. Her father, Patrick Scully, was a farmer, his wife Mary a seamstress. The Scullys were poor. Their cottage, built in the shadow of a factory, had a corrugated-iron roof, cramped rooms and few creature comforts. It was the sort of place a young girl with dreams would wish to flee from as soon as opportunity presented itself. So many Irish countrywomen had lived and died unable to better themselves. Catherine Scully was determined not to follow their example.

She left Nurney at eighteen, travelled north and enrolled at the polytechnic in Coleraine, close to Derry City – it would later undergo a change in academic status and become the University of Ulster. Catherine Scully's course of choice was one in modelling and deportment: a modern-day finishing school, you might say. It was a good choice for a girl wishing to make an impression and – it must be said – to attract the sort of man Catherine was looking for.

She started work as a receptionist in the Castle Hotel, Dublin. Whether she sought them out or not we do not know but it was at this time that she met members of Republican groups. She began to fraternize with the IRA.

This was sexy and daring; no doubt about it. For the young woman born under a tin roof in County Kildare, consorting with men who lived outside the law and were involved in a "cause" was thoroughly romantic. Life was acquiring a cachet.

A romance of another kind was in the offing too. Tom Nevin walked into the hotel one evening, and into Catherine's life.

Like her he had a farming background, though a somewhat more prosperous one. He came from Tynagh in County Galway and was a giant of a man, standing six foot three in his socks, with the build of a rugby international. But big though he was, he was a gentle soul, industrious, caring – and uncomplaining when the going was rough. He'd left home at sixteen to seek his fortune in England, finding work a-plenty in the Irish bars. He met and wed June, with whom he emigrated to Australia, where he also worked as a barman. The marriage failed and was annulled in 1970. When he met Catherine he was employed as a bar manager and was tipped to go on to greater things.

If he had a fault it was his drinking. His intake of alcohol was prodigious even then; just before his death he was putting away two pints of whiskey a day, an amount that might have destroyed a man of slighter frame. He seems to have coped, though, as many alcoholics do; his drinking wasn't going to stand in the way of his ambition.

It may be cruel to say that Catherine fell in love not with the man but with his prospects. Yet in light of what was to come it's hard to separate the loving Ms Scully from the conniving one. Be that as it may, a romance blossomed; Tom proposed marriage and they went to Rome for the ceremony. The wedding took place in January 1976. Tom Nevin was thirty-five, Catherine Scully twenty-five.

She had hotel experience; he was a professional bar manager. They decided to pool their expertise and open a pub. For some reason Catherine quizzed a Republican, John Jones, on the availability of suitable premises. He said he was unable to help in that quarter. Eventually the couple managed to secure a lease on The Barry House in Finglas, Dublin. It was somehow inevitable, given Catherine's penchant for IRA men, that before too long the pub acquired the reputation of being a Republican den.

The Nevins prospered. So well did their fortunes expand that they were buying valuable property in Dublin. By 1986 they owned two houses: one in Rialto and one in Kilmainham. It was time to consolidate.

The Nevins bought Jack White's, an inn on the Dublin to Wexford road, for IR£270,000 – a huge sum at the time. But it seemed to be worth it. It was prime property, hard by the seaside resort of Brittas Bay, ideally situated to catch the busy carriage trade between the capital and Rosslare. Tom and Catherine signed for joint ownership.

It was a decision that would prove significant in their relationship.

While Catherine enjoyed the idea of being co-proprietor of a thriving concern like Jack White's, her real interest lay in the beauty business. She'd already experimented with a model agency and beauty academy but nothing had come of it. For all that, the beauty trade, with its superficiality and veneer, suited her temperament. It also went some way towards affirming her self-image. She was certainly not plain, but neither was she a stunning beauty.

She set about expanding the inn to include a hairdressing salon and a tanning shop. But she soon discovered that business was slower than she'd hoped. White's might have a lively turnover thanks largely to its male customers, but the number of women likely to avail of the beauty parlour was too few to justify Catherine's undivided attention. She left the business in the care of an employee or two and threw herself into what she did best: looking after the customers in the bar and restaurant. Very soon she made this her domain. She was the ideal innkeeper, the perfect hostess.

At this point the good folk in the Brittas Bay area were beginning to appreciate that Catherine Nevin was no ordinary pub owner. There's a medical condition known as Narcissistic Personality Disorder by which the patient develops a highly inflated opinion of herself, craves admiration, lacks empathy with others and exploits subordinates mercilessly. Catherine seems to have been suffering from some such disorder – and was delusional into the bargain. She let it be known she had important contacts within the IRA. At first no one took her seriously, until she mentioned one important Republican by name. What's more, she claimed to have seen this gentleman threatening somebody with a gun in the carpark of Jack White's. If the inn's regulars dismissed it as another of Catherine's fantasies, the Gardaí did not.

Jack White's was a favourite of the Arklow police. It was a handy stopping-off place and a number of Guards would frequent it when either on or off duty. One such Guard pricked up his ears at the mention by name of "Catherine's" IRA man. He was unknown to all but a few. So how could the inn's new owner know him? The Garda alerted Special Branch. Jack White's came under the surveillance of the cream of the Irish detective force.

It would emerge that Catherine Nevin had – quite literally – strange bedfellows.

Tom Nevin must have suspected even during their courtship that his wife would never be satisfied with just one man. We do not know of her sexual past prior to their marriage – Catherine remained tight-lipped about this – but we know that her extra-marital affairs began after the Nevins took over Jack White's.

Catherine was a social climber *par excellence*. She'd made certain to invite as many of the local dignitaries as she could to the opening party. There were doctors, lawyers, clergymen, bankers – and two highly significant individuals: Garda Inspector Tom Kennedy and Judge Donnchadh Ó Buachalla. Their names merit watching, for they were to play decisive parts in the life of Catherine Nevin.

They represented the thing she loved most: power.

Like many people born into humble circumstances Catherine sought power and influence to make up for the shortfall. She realized from an early age that for a rural Irish girl without means there was one fast track to achieving high status: it involved making use of her looks and her sex. She was going to put into practice the valuable lessons she'd learned in Coleraine.

She must have known that Tom Nevin was destined to rise so far and no further. He was ambitious, yes, but his ambitions paled next to hers. He'd have been content with watching the fortunes of Jack White's increase steadily year by year. He was happy accumulating more and more property in Dublin, to be rented out to an ever-lengthening register of tenants. In the early 1980s property ownership in and around the capital was growing into a corpulent cash cow. One particular building lies off the South Circular Road and the Nevins had let it out in flats. No doubt Tom saw them in their twilight years selling up and enjoying a well-earned retirement on the proceeds of their little empire.

But Catherine wanted a good deal more than that. Their purchase of the inn at Brittas Bay coincided with the spectacular flowering of the Irish economy. The country saw itself acquiring a status that a decade earlier was unthinkable. Fortunes were being made to right and left of the Nevins. Catherine wanted a piece of the action, and she was coming to the realization that her husband might not be the stepping-stone to riches he'd first appeared to be.

He might even be a liability.

In hindsight it's all too easy to conjecture that Catherine's plan was a well-laid one, one she'd hit upon more than ten years before its eventual execution. Whatever the truth, the plot was to involve a man named Willie McClean.

McClean and she had met sometime around the end of 1984 in the Red Cow Inn on the Naas Road, on the outskirts of Dublin City. Catherine was attracted to his wild ways. He was not a Republican, however, but almost the antithesis: a Protestant, from County Monaghan. When the two met he was no stranger to the police or the courts. He had three criminal convictions: two for deception and fraud in the North, one for writing a dud cheque in the South. His business affairs included the highly lucrative smuggling of contraband from one jurisdiction to the other: spirits, cigarettes, laundered green diesel – wherever a good turnover lay.

He was a small-time crook, though, who worked alone. His illegal activities augmented a legitimate income derived from his skip-removal business. He would ply the building sites, offering his services where needed. At the same time he was having a vigorous sexual relationship with Catherine Nevin.

When the Nevins opened Jack White's in 1986 Willie McClean was a regular customer. He'd come and stay the weekend, and in return for board and lodgings help out behind the bar. The affair ended in 1987, but Catherine would contact Willie again almost twelve years later. She was in St Vincent's Hospital, Dublin, recovering from what Willie was given to believe was a heart attack. At her bedside she made a most unusual request – she asked him to murder her husband for her.

"There's twenty thousand punt in it for you," she said. "Get rid of Tom and you and I can get back together. What do you say, Willie?"

"I say go and fuck yourself, Catherine." But he was thoughtful for a moment; she seemed serious enough. "Where would this happen?' he asked carefully.

She had it all worked out. McClean was to "hit" Tom either going to the bank with the takings from the inn, or by lying in wait for him at the flats the couple owned off the South Circular Road.

Willie wasn't buying into it and said so. But she didn't give up, and approached him a few weeks later with a similar proposition. Again he refused. She began her quest for another likely assassin.

In the meantime she'd been making life exciting for a select group of men, and making life hell for people lower down the pecking order. From the very first days of the Jack White's venture, Catherine Nevin had made damned sure that her underlings knew who was in control. She was bossy in the extreme – as many who suddenly acquire power over others tend to be.

There was her treatment of Kathleen Stafford, a single mother who worked part-time, cleaning and doing other menial jobs. Catherine laid down "rules" that were so strict they verged on the inhumane. For example, Kathleen was to present herself at the inn early in the morning when an early start was unnecessary. Nothing she did was right. Catherine would demand that she clean again a room or rooms the young woman had already cleaned thoroughly.

The crunch came when Kathleen refused to work full-time. She couldn't; she had a child to rear. But, according to author Niamh O'Connor, Catherine allegedly shopped her to the social welfare and an inspector called to her humble home to investigate. (This is surely a measure of the climate that prevailed in late-eighties Ireland. The state was willing to invest the time of a well-paid official in order to recover what may have amounted to small change earned – but undeclared – by a poor cleaner, while at the same time fortunes were being shunted to offshore accounts by certain members of Charles Haughey's "golden circle". No wonder cynics would refer to the "Celtic Rat" as opposed to the much-vaunted "Celtic Tiger".)

Eileen Byrne fared no better than Kathleen. The pensioner likewise worked for Catherine on a part-time basis. By all accounts she was a good, conscientious worker. Not good enough for the mistress of Jack White's, though. Catherine treated her most shabbily. Matters came to a head when Eileen refused to clean for the second time mirrors that were spotless. Catherine sacked her.

The staff loathed her. Stories were emerging all the time of her tyrannical rule, about people being put out onto the street at midnight for the tiniest infraction of the "rules".

Nor was her abuse confined to those who worked for her. She reported the theft of cigarettes to the Arklow police. Two Guards came to investigate, but Catherine was upset, thinking – wrongly – that they weren't taking the theft seriously enough. She embarked on a campaign to ruin their careers, displaying a vindictiveness to rival Queen Jezebel's.

At the other end of the scale, however, were the people whose favours Catherine was doing her best to curry. One was Tom Kennedy, a Garda inspector attached to Arklow station. His was the most senior rank in the area and it was probably for this reason that Catherine was attracted to him. Although Kennedy was later to deny it in court, there were a number of witnesses who swore they became intimate in or around 1991. Kennedy retired from the force in 1994 and a party was held in his honour in Jack White's.

But Catherine was reaching higher up the social ladder. Through Tom Kennedy she met Judge Donnchadh Ó Buachalla, who was likewise to deny that he'd had an "irregular sexual relationship" with her. This went directly against the evidence of two former employees of hers, who insisted that not only was the judge intimate with her but that he even had his own key to the premises.

In effect Tom and Catherine Nevin had stopped living as husband and wife as early as 1986. By 1989 there was nothing left of their sex life, and very little of their marriage. She wanted out. She wanted a divorce. Tom refused time and again to agree to one. It would be more than his mother could take, he argued. One annulled marriage was enough.

Tom Nevin was getting in the way of the life Catherine had envisaged for herself. He had to go. The big mistake the big man had made was to have the property the couple owned registered in both their names. Catherine wanted it all, and said so. She threatened her husband with murder. He didn't think she was capable of such a thing.

He should have believed her.

Between 1989 and 1991 Catherine made no fewer than eighteen requests to have her husband disposed of. She made them of three men. The first was Willie McClean; the second was John Jones.

To place Jones chronologically in the Nevin saga we must go back to Finglas, Dublin, and the year 1984. At this time Catherine and Tom Nevin were still finding their feet in the hospitality trade. The pub they were running, The Barry House, was living up to its reputation of bidding welcome to Republicans, and John Jones was one of the regulars.

He was born in 1944 in Balbriggan. In the 1980s he ran a TV rentals shop in Finglas. He was also the chairman of the local Sinn Féin *cumann* and hosted an SF advice centre in his shop. It was inevitable he should gravitate to The Barry House and befriend the Nevins, although he'd met Catherine earlier when she called at his shop to ask his advice on licensed premises she might buy. When the Nevins took over the lease to the pub Catherine invited Jones to hold Republican meetings and fundraising evenings there. She thought she'd earn political kudos that way, and she was not mistaken. Perhaps what endeared her to Jones most, however, was that she put business his way, at one time renting a sound system and two television sets from him.

When the Nevins moved out of the area and to Brittas Bay they lost touch with Jones. Until one day in 1989 Catherine returned unexpectedly to the TV rental shop. She had a proposition for him, she said. This time it involved neither electronics nor Republican evenings. She wondered if he might do her a favour and dispatch her husband.

"I want you to get the IRA to shoot Tom," she said, "and make it look like it was a robbery."

"Would you ever fuck off, Catherine," he said with a smile, effectively echoing Willie McClean. He too thought she was joking.

But she returned a few weeks later – and left Jones in no doubt of her sincerity. She'd worked out a plan. It was, she said, to be put into effect that coming bank-holiday weekend, when the takings from Jack White's would be in excess of £25,000. Tom would be taking the cash to his bank in Dublin. All the IRA had to do was waylay him, kill him and make off with the money.

Simple.

But John Jones wouldn't hear of it. He was proud of the IRA and his membership thereof. What did she think they were, common thugs and murderers?

"No," he said. "No way."

He kept on saying it, for Catherine was to ask him again and again in the eighteen months that followed. She hounded him in his shop; she badgered him in his home in Balbriggan.

Once she called into his Sinn Féin advice centre with bandaged hands and wrists, and what looked to Jones like two black eyes. Tom had beaten her up, she said. Would he reconsider and do away with him for her? (What she neglected to tell Jones was that the bandages and bruising were the result of cosmetic surgery she'd undergone. All told, the vain Catherine would have eighteen procedures, ranging from liposuction to an eyelift.)

Still John Jones refused to go along with Tom's murder. She turned to another: Gerry Heapes.

On the face of it, Heapes was a rather pathetic figure. Born in 1950, he grew up in working-class Finglas. He joined the IRA and participated in a number of their fundraising armed robberies in the 1970s. Following one such heist, at Leyden's Cash & Carry on Richmond Road, Fairview, he was arrested and sentenced to ten years in jail. He gained early release for good behaviour in 1985, and joined the Jack McCabe *cumann* of Sinn Féin that same year. He was well liked. The *cumann* raised £225 for him and this helped him get back on his feet again – after a fashion. His IRA activities and criminal record were working against him; Heapes had little hope of finding a job, and had a wife to support. He was reduced to tracing shamrocks and Republican symbols onto handkerchiefs to be sold in America, this cottage industry being pursued in a back room off John Jones's advice centre.

It was Jones who introduced him to Catherine Nevin, and Heapes too became a regular customer in her Finglas pub. When she opened the inn near Brittas Bay she made sure to invite him and his wife to the party. Heapes remembers Catherine greeting them in person and showing them around the gathering. He recalls that she was unusually conscious of class differences.

"There's a judge," she said, pointing out Justice Ó Buachalla, "there's an inspector, and" – said with barely restrained contempt – "that's a load of boggers over there."

Out of the blue Catherine turned up at the *cumann* office in Finglas. She invited Gerry for a drive. She had "a proposition" for him. She stopped the car in the Phoenix Park and cut the engine.

"Can you murder my husband?" she asked a shocked Gerry Heapes.

She'd worked out a plan. As in the case of the proposition she'd put to John Jones, the plan would take advantage of the coming bank-holiday weekend. Again the takings from Jack White's would exceed £25,000 and Tom would be taking the cash to his Dublin bank. Gerry and his IRA accomplices were to kill and rob him. She'd worked it all out. It was foolproof, she said.

Gerry's first thought was that it was, as he put it, "a wind-up". But it wasn't, as he soon began to appreciate. Catherine was deadly serious.

"Twenty-five thousand isn't worth a person's life," he told her.

She let the matter rest for the time being. A few weeks later she was in touch again, and he agreed to meet her in the same place. Again she offered £25,000.

"Nobody would do it for that kind of money," he assured her.

Catherine was no fool. She recalled a contract killing in Limerick less than a decade before. Declan Malone had accepted a mere £200 for shooting Majella Boland's husband. But Malone was a dissident Republican and Heapes a Provo; Catherine was beginning to understand that the IRA's "tariffs" were higher.

"What are we talking about then?" she asked.

Humouring her, Heapes explained patiently that it couldn't be a one-man operation. There'd have to be motorbikes and cars and guns. A lot of planning and a lot of expense. She thought about it. She raised the price, and also agreed to a payment "up front".

Then there was the matter of the location. Catherine took Heapes to the first she'd earmarked for the hit: a block of flats the Nevins owned. Heapes dismissed it. Too dangerous; no escape route. She next drove him to The Grasshopper pub in Clonee, where Tom would normally stop off.

Heapes kept on telling her that he'd "think about it" and she kept on returning to visit him in Finglas. In the end she accepted his reluctance for what it was: a gentle refusal. If Tom Nevin were to die then it would not be by the hand of Willie McClean, or John Jones, or Gerry Heapes.

But die he did: on or about three in the morning of 19 March 1996, and by an unknown hand. Catherine had finally managed to engage the services of her assassin for hire.

We do not know how much money changed hands prior to the murder, nor what the total was at the job's completion. It seems reasonable to assume, however, that it exceeded £25,000. Whether the fee went to a lone gunman or a group will probably never be known for certain. But in all likelihood the killer was working alone.

The takings from Jack White's would have been substantial. It was the St Patrick's Day weekend, which began on the Friday. The previous day's trade, on 14 March, had netted £4,500. In the ordinary run of things, Tom would have taken this to his bank in Wicklow town. The same bank would have given him a number of bags of coins, the small change needed for the cash registers at the inn, in preparation for the weekend. He didn't reach the bank in time, though, because Catherine stalled him. She persuaded him instead to drive her to her doctor to collect a prescription. Once there, she deliberately delayed, causing Tom to miss the lodgment. The £4,500 would be added to the bank-holiday weekend takings.

On Monday, at about six in the evening, a stranger in a long dark coat entered the inn and ordered coffee in the lounge. It was noted that he made a whispered phone call. No one saw him leave.

There was the customary Monday-night disco in Arklow. Normally the staff of Jack White's would go there by minibus and afterwards spend the night back at the inn. Not this time. There were other arrangements, Catherine announced; they could all go to their own homes. If they'd "no homes to go to" she didn't care. In the restaurant she ordered the curtains drawn and the tables cleared before ten. Again this was out of the ordinary. If she wished to arouse the suspicions of the staff she was going the right way about it.

But in fact she was intent on calling attention to herself; this evening she was going out of her way to impress. She wished to make it abundantly clear that Jack White's – and Catherine Nevin herself – were prime targets for anybody contemplating a robbery. She went to her bedroom and fetched out her jewellery box. By 1996 its contents were quite valuable indeed; hence its hiding place in the bottom of her closet. No one but she knew of its existence, not even Tom. Her precious rings, gold crucifix and other baubles were safe – especially from the detested lowly members of staff. She removed them from their place of concealment. She festooned herself with enough gold ornament to put a Marrakesh harlot to shame. When she swept into the bar in a mink coat, expensive scent trailing behind her, all heads turned – as was her intention. The faces betrayed what many were surely thinking: *That one's worth robbing . . .*

The minibus departed for the disco a little after midnight. Some minutes later the last of the patrons had left Jack White's. No one remained except Tom Nevin and his wife. She went to bed, leaving him alone in the kitchen.

We have only Catherine Nevin's version of events to account for what occurred in the early hours of the morning. From what detectives could piece together, the following scenario may be close to what actually took place.

At a pre-arranged time Catherine went to a bedroom and spoke quietly to the man she'd hired to dispatch her husband. It's safe to assume he was indeed already on the premises. They could have faked a forced entry but decided not to, the killer probably having cautioned against it. A professional would know that the Guards have a happy knack of seeing through such deception.

Tom Nevin hadn't a prayer. He was perched on a stool at the kitchen workbench, going over his finances. We don't know if Catherine accompanied his assassin when he entered with a shotgun, a fowling piece. Let us hope for his sake that she did not, that Tom believed he was about to be attacked by a common thief and that his own wife had no hand in the killing. One shot, fired at close range and entering his chest, was sufficient. Tom would have died within seconds.

When the Gardaí found him later that morning he was lying on the floor, still wearing his reading glasses. On the workbench was a half-empty glass of Guinness, his final drink.

In order for the plan to work, it had to be shown that Catherine too was a victim. She therefore allowed herself to be "surprised" in her bedroom. She was tied to a chair and gagged. It was plausible enough: the thief would have seen her jewellery, scooped it up and set off in search of further loot.

She was to say that a hooded man brandishing a knife had burst into her room, tied her up and made off with her jewellery. From her room she'd heard shouts, and a loud noise in another part of the house. It had sounded like "a saucepan" falling to the floor. The gunshot. She then heard two cars driving off at speed.

The thieves must indeed have panicked, because strewn from the hall to the kitchen was a trail of Catherine's stolen jewellery. She claims to have reached a panic button in the hall and summoned the Guards. They arrived at 4.27 a.m.

There was no sign of course of the murderer but £13,000 was missing: the takings from Jack White's. The total "haul", including the £4,500 from Friday, was never established.

She might have got away with it. She might have inherited Tom's half of the estate, cashed in his life insurance policies and emerged from the affair a millionaire. Unfortunately for her she'd made too many enemies among the people she'd always regarded as unimportant. Now they turned on her.

They reported that prior to the shooting they'd heard the couple arguing and Catherine issuing death threats. She'd mentioned the IRA. To be sure, married couples do argue heatedly at times and may threaten each other in the white heat of anger. But Catherine had made no secret of her association with the IRA. She was on the contrary inordinately proud of her relations with high-ups in the organization.

At the same time, the police investigation was concentrating on the murder scene, how the body was found – and the events leading up to the fatal shooting. There were so many inconsistencies in her story that finally, on 28 July 1996, she was arrested and taken to Enniscorthy Garda station. She refused to answer any questions and was detained overnight. Next day she was more forthcoming.

They wished to know how it was she'd heard the gunshot when forensic tests proved that this was impossible. They wished to know how a man can topple from a high stool and still be wearing his reading glasses. They wished to know why she drew the curtains in the restaurant and sent all the staff packing. There were questions concerning the keys to Jack White's, an open door, her jewellery, the fact that her ankles didn't appear to have been bound as she'd stated. Questions that Catherine could not answer.

She was charged with the murder of her husband and sent to trial on 12 January 2000. By this time all her assets had been frozen. Tom Nevin's family were determined she wouldn't get her hands on any of his property. She'd almost succeeded, thanks to Judge Donnchadh Ó Buachalla, who arranged for the licence on Jack White's to be renewed solely in her name following her husband's murder. An inquiry found that the judge had made "an error of judgement". It was all to no avail; she could do nothing with the property or any of the other assets she'd shared with Tom. She was virtually penniless. The woman who'd flown so high was reduced to seeking legal aid.

But what a defendant she made! Catherine, to the delight of the media, presented herself each morning meticulously turned out, hair freshly done, a different outfit nearly every day. If the country was watching then she'd give the country plenty to watch.

The trial was doomed, though. Fourteen days into the session in the High Court it had to be aborted. The court crier claimed that the walls of the jury room were so thin he could plainly hear the case being discussed.

A second trial was mounted but this too had to be stopped when a jury member fell ill.

The third trial had to be adjourned when the defendant herself declared she was unwell. She wasn't. She was faking it. When the trial resumed six days later, it was found that Catherine made an unusually poor witness. It was obvious she was lying about so many aspects of the affair. The notes of the trial record showed nearly one hundred contradictions in the evidence she gave during the four days she was on the stand. Her testimony turned truly farcical when she claimed that Tom had been a member of the IRA.

The court heard about her many and myriad medical complaints. A tissue of lies. Most of her hospital admissions were for cosmetic surgery. She'd even told the staff of St Vincent's Hospital she was undergoing chemotherapy. Baron Münchausen, the fantasist, would have been proud of her.

The prosecution had called nearly two hundred witnesses, including Catherine's three potential hit-men: Willie McClean, John Jones and Gerry Heapes. A shocked nation learned how all three had been propositioned. The evidence was stacked against Catherine. None could doubt that she was guilty, and the third jury did indeed on 11 April 2000 find her guilty of murder. Justice Mella Carroll would sentence her on four counts: for the killing of her husband and for three times soliciting a man to do just that. She handed down a mandatory life sentence, to begin at once in Mountjoy Prison, Dublin. On 7 June the judge gave her three consecutive sentences of seven years each for soliciting to murder.

Men die for all sorts of reasons: some good, some brave, some noble. Tom Nevin died for two wholly inappropriate reasons. Had Catherine Nevin not been greedy and callous he'd doubtless be alive today. But there was another factor that hastened his departure from this life: he felt that a divorce would cause his mother too much grief. He'd already made her suffer the ignominy attached in rural Ireland to a failed marriage and a decree of annulment. Catherine wanted a divorce. That was one separation too far.

Catherine Nevin appealed her life sentence in March 2003. Again it was a female judge who presided: Justice Mary Finlay-Geoghegan. While the hearing itself lasted a week, the judge's decision needed only moments to voice.

"We refuse leave to appeal," she declared.

Catherine tried again in 2009, but at the time of writing there seems no prospect yet of her even being granted parole.

And Jack White's Inn? After the trial in 2000 it enjoyed more prosperity than Catherine could have foreseen. Even during the court proceedings it had become a Mecca for the curious. The new owners are reaping the rewards of its notoriety; years after the event business is still booming. There are visitors who make sure to keep their bar receipts as grisly mementoes. Others have their photograph taken with the pub sign in the background. There are even those who ask to see Catherine's bedroom.

She was received into Mountjoy Jail, Dublin, in time to occupy a cell in the new female wing, built at a cost of 16 million and opened in 1999. Known as the Dóchas Centre – *dóchas* is the Irish for "hope" – it's a far cry from Mountjoy's old "female prison" with its "seventy women", as immortalized in song by Brendan Behan.

The cells are in fact rooms and there are no bars on the windows. The room's occupant holds her own key to her door and is free to come and go as she pleases – within the prison – until 7.30 p.m. Her room overlooks a pleasant garden with trees, shrubs and flowers, and has an en-suite bathroom – at odds with the metal in-cell toilets in the men's wing of Mountjoy and other Irish jails. In fact, the female prisoner's room, with its tasteful décor and furnishings, would not look out of place in an ordinary home. This is deliberate policy; the emphasis here is not on punishment but rehabilitation. The Centre is in stark contrast to Limerick women's prison, the country's other facility, with its harsh regime, its two-to-a-cell policy and a distinct lack of anything approaching comfort. Privacy is non-existent: according to the Irish Prisons Inspectorate, it's "cramped, very confined and claustrophobic". It's a lock-up jail: the inmates are confined to their cells for eighteen hours out of every twenty-four. Limerick is also where those women who abuse the privileges of Dóchas are sent.

"We are a community which embraces people with respect and dignity," the Centre's mission statement reads. "We encourage personal growth in a caring and safe environment. We are committed to addressing the needs of each person in a healing and holistic way. We actively promote close interaction with the wider community."

The Dóchas Centre is, in short, a model prison, unlike anything else here or in Britain. There are seven separate houses, each of which bears the name of a tree. It resembles more than anything a college campus – it even has its own school that offers everything from computer lessons to English to photography and pottery classes. Swimming and hillwalking are actively encouraged. There's also a fine gym and a hair and beauty salon. A first-class health centre provides medical and dental care.

It's commonly said that jail "is no picnic". In the case of Dóchas, however, this is not always true. In 2004 news leaked out that a party of inmates, among them Ireland's most notorious female criminals, had been driven to Dollymount beach in north Dublin for a picnic. For four hours the ladies enjoyed tea and sandwiches, sweets and soft drinks while day-trippers looked on bemused.

Yet despite these unique amenities Catherine Nevin did not take well to prison life. In the beginning it was making her physically ill, her lawyer reported: she'd developed a kidney complaint and was utterly miserable. Nor did she mix, either with staff or prisoners, apart from two South Americans doing time for drug smuggling. Her first Christmas in Dóchas was a lonely one as well; she was the only inmate without visitors.

In 2008 she was caught in possession of a mobile phone; if found guilty of the offence she could face a large fine or have her sentence extended further. She remains hopeful, however, that her days in Mountjoy are numbered. At the time of going to press, she and her legal staff are applying to the Court of Criminal Appeal to have her conviction overturned. She remains adamant that a new trial would prove her innocence and that she's the victim of a miscarriage of justice.

We shall see. In the meantime Catherine consoles herself with writing poetry. The prison magazine was proud to publish the following lines from the hand of the Black Widow.

> *Being a good friend is really an art,*
> *A wonderful talent that comes from the heart.*
> *It's knowing the kind of thing to do or say,*
> *Listening and talking a problem away.*
> *It's caring for someone, and showing it too,*
> *Thank goodness for friends, friends just like you.*

4

KATHLEEN BELL
Child Abuse is no Laughing Matter

The sexual abuse of a child is one of the vilest crimes imaginable. The victim's view of adults and the world changes for ever; true childhood is suspended, if not snuffed out; life can never be "normal" again.

Laurie Pearlman, a Connecticut psychologist who works with traumatized children, believes that sexual abuse will colour all a child's relationships. "To be used as an object to satisfy someone else's need," she says, "is a profound violation of the self." A child is left asking: "Whom can I trust? Can I trust myself? Am I a worthy person or simply an object to be used by others? Am I valuable? Can I control what happens to me?"

Questions impossible for the child to answer by herself. Whom can she turn to? Without answers or an adult to help, Pearlman maintains, a child may store the experience away as a secret, becoming "withdrawn, depressed or acting out, causing trouble at home or school".

The child is scarred, wounded beyond the reach of lasting healing. And the scarring can be both mental and physical. Moreover, it is sometimes inflicted by the victim herself. Such is the trauma the abuse imposes that the child will grow up in an unreal world, one in which she feels no genuine emotions: love, hate, joy, sorrow. Often she'll choose to take a knife or razor to her own body: self-harming. Each wound she traces on her arms, neck or elsewhere causes pain. This is her only means of experiencing the reality a normal person experiences on an everyday basis.

In the wake of the Ferns child-abuse scandal, Colm O'Gorman, who'd been raped by the infamous Father Sean Fortune, founded the group One in Four, first in London, later in Dublin in 2002. The name derives from statistics which suggest that one in four Irish and British children will be abused at some time in their lives – and those statistics derive from the cases that see the light of day.

But for Kathleen Bell and her siblings it was a case of one in two. Both she and her young sister Mary suffered sexual abuse. It was to mar their lives, and leave the adult Kathleen with the mental age of an eight-year-old – a woman barely responsible for her own actions. In the words of a social worker she was a "very damaged individual".

The damage would be measurable too. Sexual abuse can actually damage the brain itself. Studies have shown that the hippocampus – a region of the brain responsible for our emotional functioning – can, in an abused woman, be five per cent smaller than in those who've had a normal childhood. The earlier the abuse, the less developed this part of the brain will be.

To say that such a victim is "scarred for life" is no exaggeration.

Kathleen was born in Galway in 1962. Her father was a busker; he was also a wife-beater and hopeless alcoholic. Having soured her life, he deserted his spouse, leaving her penniless with four children to look after: two boys and two girls. Perhaps worse still, Kathleen's father bequeathed his drink problem to his daughter. It would eventually lead to her downfall – and to the untimely and violent death of a man three decades on, in 1997.

With the father gone, and the mother unable to cope, the three youngest children were committed into the care of orphanages: one in Galway, the other in Moate, County Westmeath.

While the vast majority of orphanage staff lavish care and affection on the home's disadvantaged children, it's a sad fact of life that such institutions will on occasion attract individuals whose motives for being close to minors are less than honourable. The orphanage in Moate harboured such a one – in this case a woman. Kathleen and her sister Mary were sexually abused by this unnamed individual. The trauma she inflicted on the girls was to have far-reaching consequences.

When Kathleen was ten, a Dublin couple arranged to take the abandoned sisters each weekend. It was a very charitable act, and Kathleen seemed at first blush to have been given the opportunity of forgetting the abuse she'd suffered in Moate. But her relief was short-lived. It ended when a close relative of the family raped her. Not once but often. The violations would become a part of Kathleen's life. One such rape resulted in a pregnancy, and a daughter was born to Kathleen when she was sixteen. The infant was taken away from her immediately after the birth. The blow was devastating.

"She was all I had," Kathleen said.

Yet her life appeared to have turned a corner when in 1980 she met and fell in love with a Derryman named Philip Bell. She became pregnant by him. They married the following year and set up home in Newcastle, County Galway. She was eighteen.

She went on to have four more children, one of whom died in infancy. Kathleen's doctor advised her against having more, and prescribed contraception. She told Philip she was "on the pill".

He had other ideas. He was a pietistic Catholic, having grown up in a staunchly religious family in the Bogside.

"There'll be no contraception in my house!" he said.

"It's me who has to have the babies, Phil, not you," Kathleen countered. "And it's me who has to raise them too."

"Right," he said darkly, "we'll see about that."

He beat her almost senseless.

71

Next day she was astonished to find that her brutal husband had enlisted the support of the parish priest, whom he brought to the house: an ally of authority and standing. Kathleen would be cured of her wayward ways. If the priest saw Kathleen's bruises and black eye he neglected to pass comment on them. After all, women were inclined to walk into doors when their minds were elsewhere, weren't they?

The good Father reminded her that contraception was evil. Had Pope Paul VI not circulated his encyclical *Humanae Vitae* to that effect in 1968? Had the pontiff not declared contraception to be contrary to God's design and "could open wide the way for marital infidelity and a general lowering of moral standards"? He had. Kathleen must continue to bear children, the priest declared. It was God's will.

Matters reached a head the following year when Philip spent their last £40 on an elaborate holy-water font. And this at a time when, in Kathleen's words, "there was no bread in the house".

Her marriage was doomed; that much she knew. One of them had to go: she or Philip. He solved the problem by leaving her and the children – there were six now – in Galway and going to England to look for work. Left penniless, as her mother was, and with children of her own to care for, Kathleen suffered a nervous breakdown. Social services intervened, taking the children into care. One was put up for adoption. History was repeating itself.

It was all too much for Kathleen. She took an overdose of pills, ending up in nearby Ballinasloe hospital, alive but emotionally scarred.

Philip Bell learned of the circumstances. He returned to County Galway and demanded custody of his children, and succeeded. He had his marriage annulled by the Catholic Church, and returned to Derry, taking the children with him. He was to remarry in 1997.

Kathleen had nothing. No family, no husband, no money, no life. She was on the downward slope. She began to self-harm, ending up in hospital on a number of occasions.

Hospitals were to figure frequently in her life.

Meanwhile her sister Mary, a woman no less damaged by her background and sexual abuse suffered in childhood, had found what she'd hoped would be a better life. She met a man, fell in love, and had a child by him. They split up soon after the birth. In 1984 she met Patrick Sammon, a fellow native of Galway, and all seemed well. They married and had three children together.

Yet the old demons that haunted her big sister were plaguing Mary too. In hindsight Pat Sammon was a disaster in the making. He was a shiftless individual. He was also an alcoholic and a wife-beater. To make matters even worse he was a gambler; what little housekeeping money they had went on the horses. In short there were eerie echoes of the sisters' feckless father – it seems that those traits that made their mother's life a misery were to follow them through life.

Mary finally plucked up the courage to leave her husband. In 1988 she moved to London, taking her children with her. Like her sister, however, Mary was a damaged individual, suffering from chronic depression. She sought solace in drugs. Relatively harmless ones at first: cannabis and the odd ecstasy tablet. But soon she was doing the harder drugs. Finally her addiction grew so bad that social services had to intervene. They took her children into care.

In the meantime, back in Galway, Patrick Sammon had begun an affair with Mary's sister. By 1994 their relationship had developed to the extent that they decided to set up house together.

But Patrick was no ordinary lover. He was a very abusive and violent man. He beat Kathleen so badly that she had to be hospitalized. In all, she paid fifty-one visits to the emergency ward; Patrick was responsible for almost as many of those visits as was her self-harming. Often their rows were so vicious that Kathleen would order him out of the house and he'd spend a night or two in a hostel.

"Patrick was the best man in the world without a drink," Kathleen recalls (thereby displaying her limited acquaintance with the world's men) "but a completely different person when he was drinking."

It was only a matter of time before something gave.

Kathleen's younger sister Mary died on 18 April 1997 in Middlesex Hospital, London. She'd swallowed a cocktail of alcohol and drugs. She left behind four children, all of whom were in the care of social services. Patrick Sammon was the father of three: two boys and a little girl. The fourth child had been fathered by another.

Patrick was not to learn of Mary's death until two months had passed. His brother Willie called him from London. His response was less than sympathetic – his marriage to Mary was finally over; he could marry her sister. He also hoped to get custody of his little girl; he decided that the boys would be better off in England.

Kathleen was devastated on hearing of Mary's death. Two days had passed since the phone call from London. Patrick had come home that evening at about eleven-thirty. They were drinking cans of beer together. At last he plucked up the courage to pop the question.

She was appalled at the suggestion. Had the man no tact? Didn't he see she was grieving? But he only laughed.

"You don't give a fuck about your sister."

"That's not true! She was my own flesh and blood. We came through hell together, Mary and me."

"What, the so-called abuse? If you ask me, the two of ye enjoyed it."

He laughed again – this time viciously and cruelly.

She was incensed. "That's a rotten thing to say! And that child doesn't want to come back here. She's happy in England. They all hate you."

He lunged at her, fists balled. She backed away.

"I'll call the Guards, Patrick!"

"Call them. I don't give a fuck about the Guards."

"Well, I'm going to the toilet."

"You can go to hell for all I care," he said.

She left the room in a blaze of fury. On her way to the lavatory she picked up a knife in the kitchen. It was sharp; it was the one she used to peel potatoes. Trembling in the bathroom, she concealed the knife under her sweater.

But when she returned to the living-room Patrick was still drunk and in a blind rage. He lunged at her again. Frightened, she produced the knife. The sight of the weapon stopped him in his tracks.

"Will you just get out, Patrick?" she implored him. "I just want you to go!"

"I'm not fucking going anywhere. Oh, go on: blame me for the kids. I suppose I'm to blame for your sister's death too, am I? She was a fucking drug addict. She was an accident waiting to happen. A useless bitch. A waste of fucking space."

Kathleen lost control. She was no longer thinking coherently. Patrick had insulted poor, dead Mary once too often. She lunged with the knife.

"I freaked out," she recalled later. "It was happening so fast. I didn't know what I was doing."

She drove the knife into his chest and he went down. Such was the force of the thrust that the momentum carried Kathleen forward. She sprawled on top of the fallen man. Driven mad by fear and loathing, she stabbed him five more times.

He did not get up.

"Pat, stop messing."

He didn't budge.

The horror of her act was coming home to Kathleen. It was real. She had stabbed a man to death.

She panicked, dropping the knife.

She knocked on the door of Bernard Ward, a neighbour and friend, and told him that Patrick was lying dead in their home. Ward called the Gardaí. She tried to blame the crime on another. When a detective sergeant arrived she stated that Sammon had returned home with a knife wound, which he claimed had been inflicted by an unknown assailant. However, within minutes of the lie, Kathleen broke down and admitted her guilt.

"I didn't mean to kill Pat!" she wailed to the Gardaí who arrested her. "I lost the head. I freaked out."

The case came to trial on 9 March 1999 in the Central Criminal Court, Dublin.

Kathleen Bell cut a pathetic figure. Small of stature, overweight and with an unhealthy pallor, she could not fail to elicit compassion from judge and jury alike. Nevertheless the prosecution put their case that this was no instance of self-defence – the defendant had used considerable force to stab Pat Sammon to death. They claimed that she'd set out to murder him.

There was blame on both sides. Both Kathleen and Pat were heavy drinkers – and violent. It seems that Kathleen gave almost as good as she got because the injuries he received from her during their drunken bouts of violence sent him to hospital on several occasions.

But it was no equal fight. Kathleen had been hospitalized a score of times following beatings by Sammon. On one occasion he'd assaulted her when she was pregnant. Three days later she'd miscarried. The court heard a sad litany of abuse and battering.

It must have seemed odd to the jury and those others present in the courtroom as the trial progressed – it was to last for more than a fortnight – that Kathleen Bell had teamed up with Pat Sammon in the first place. This was, after all, the man who'd grossly mistreated her sister. One explanation is that female victims of sexual abuse in childhood develop a dependency on the male. There's a condition known as Dependent Personality Disorder. The sufferer is overly submissive and has an excessive need to be taken care of. Psychiatrists and social workers see it all too often in victims of abuse. It could be compared to the so-called Stockholm syndrome seen in hostages. More often than not the woman is drawn to a man having traits similar to those of her abuser. It's as if she's choosing the devil she knows rather than a threat that's new – and all the more menacing for that. The unfamiliar can be frightening to a woman with the mental age of eight.

Yet the jury heard from Kathleen's own lips that she loved Pat Sammon and he loved her. Despite their frequent quarrels, despite the savage beatings she suffered at his hands – and indeed feet, and knives, and once with a heavy kettle – they could be a devoted couple. They'd even planned to marry.

But all this would change when Pat informed her of the death of her sister. His callousness proved too much for Kathleen.

There could be little doubt in the minds of all present in the court throughout the trial that they were dealing with an unusually damaged person. They heard from Kathleen's own lips and from a number of witnesses – both expert and lay – that her life had been a chain of misfortune and abuse. They heard how she'd attempted suicide in the early 1990s when her husband Philip Bell had left her and gone to England to seek work. She couldn't cope, took an overdose, and in doing so forfeited custody of the children. It seemed that Kathleen was doomed to lose the children she so much wanted. It also seemed that she consistently chose men who gave her little except grief. She needed some control over her life and circumstances. She was continually denied it. Nor could she control her own actions.

Her defence counsel reminded the jury of Mary's blighted childhood and later life. He urged them to consider the consequences the sexual abuse had had on the life of the adult. Mary was, he said, "a seriously damaged individual who had an awful life".

He emphasized the fact that the abuse was no abstract occurrence that could be confined to the past. A "real live Kathleen Bell" was systematically sexually abused and subjected to "terrible, debasing stuff". Her sense of self-worth had been destroyed – the same had happened with her sister Mary. The abuse was no laughing matter, as Patrick Sammon discovered to his cost.

She didn't have the knowledge or experience of life to deal with that taunting, a psychiatrist told the court. Her self-confidence had been undermined many years before, and continued to be undermined.

"She was trapped," he said. "There was nothing new about being trapped. She was trapped for years, but this was the apex of the mental torture and harassment."

That could very well change in the future; the damage might yet be undone – to an extent. The jury learned that from the time of her arrest Kathleen was undergoing therapy. The prognosis looked positive. There was hope of rehabilitation.

The presiding judge, Mrs Justice Catherine McGuinness, directed that the jury find her guilty of manslaughter. The jury duly returned that verdict. The judge sentenced Kathleen to four years but decided to suspend the sentence – on condition that the defendant continued to attend counselling. But there was also the problem posed by her excessive drinking. In return for her freedom Kathleen pledged to attend meetings of Alcoholics Anonymous for the duration of the suspended sentence.

And so ended the decades of suffering that had begun in childhood and had culminated in two needless deaths: that of Kathleen's sister Mary and the man she married. A social worker present during the summing-up would later comment on the succession of events that led to those lives being taken.

"That's abuse of children for you," she said. "I wonder if the people who do these things are really aware of the devastation they cause. I doubt if they are. A man who sexually abuses a child for a few minutes of selfish pleasure would never stop to think about the lives he's ruining. He's not only ruining any chance of happiness for the child, he's also putting the lives of others in jeopardy. He couldn't possibly know who the others are because they're a long way in the future. The people who abused Kathleen Bell and her sister as good as killed Patrick Sammon."

That statement alone should give all of us pause.

5

CAROLINE COMERFORD
Mariticide in Rathfarnham

Generally speaking the Irish, north and south, have an ambivalent attitude towards alcohol. Always have, and perhaps always will. Never mind that alcohol abuse accounts for hundreds, if not thousands, of hospital deaths each year. Never mind that more than a third of fatal accidents on our roads are drink-related. In the island of Ireland alcohol is an accepted part of the culture and very few would regard it as a drug.

Yet a drug it is. It's a mind-altering substance but is seldom spoken of in those terms.

Such is the Irish tolerance of alcohol abuse that the people of Belfast could name an airport for a former footballer who died a hopeless alcoholic, and the Ulster Bank – which is permitted to issue its own currency – could immortalize its hero on a £5 note. George Best died of alcoholism, having undergone a liver transplant intended to repair the damage he'd done to his body. Instead he seems to have regarded the new organ as an excuse to continue his fatal drinking.

What if George had died a heroin addict? It would be unthinkable for an Irish airport to be dedicated to a drug slave. Yet that is precisely what the once-great sportsman was. Alcohol is a drug whose effects are devastating.

There will be no airports named for Peter Comerford. He was both a heroin addict and an alcoholic – a deadly combination. But football was Peter's undoing. Not because he played it but because he visited his local playing fields in Rathfarnham on the day of his death.

It was Sunday, 9 August 1998. He was thirty-nine; his wife Caroline was thirty-four. They had two teenaged children, a girl and boy. They also had a marriage that had been blighted by drink; Caroline too was an alcoholic.

It's unclear how much drink the pair consumed that day but it must have been an outrageous amount. Over time the alcoholic can develop a phenomenal tolerance. It's by no means uncommon for a heavy drinker to get through one or more litres of spirits and appear no more than tipsy – we shall shortly be examining the last days of Farah Noor, the African who fell foul of the Mulhall sisters, a man whose tolerance of alcohol was truly off the scale.

The Comerfords had been drinking spirits that day. A vast quantity of spirits. Caroline's sister Deborah showed up at the playing fields accompanied by her boyfriend and found the pair very drunk. No wonder. Deborah reported seeing several vodka bottles, most drained to the last drop. She also noted an unlabelled bottle, likewise empty. She sniffed it; it had contained poitín.

Poitín, Ireland's very own moonshine, is arguably the strongest intoxicating spirit in the world. It's distilled from malted barley grain, or equally often from potatoes, and has been a "poor-man's poison" for hundreds of years. Although its manufacture is generally regarded as being confined to rural areas, the capital has long enjoyed its own thriving industry. There's even a pub-restaurant called An Poitín Stil in Rathcoole, County Dublin. The Revenue Commissioners – the "excise man" in the old vernacular – banned it long ago yet in recent years there's been a change of heart. The ban was lifted in 1997, a year before the Comerfords' afternoon outing, and it went on sale legally in 2000.

The Comerfords were barely coherent when Deborah came upon them. The poitín they'd drunk was strong enough to cripple a camel; the vodka had sent them over the edge. Peter had, to his credit, managed to kick his heroin habit after more than a decade. He'd been "clean" for several months, thanks to the surrogate drug methadone.

Deborah's boyfriend drove them to their home in Carrickmount Drive, Rathfarnham, promising to call back later when they were sobered up a little. The children were out with friends. Peter, with great difficulty, mounted the stairs, intending to sleep off the combined effects of the vodka, poitín and methadone.

He could easily have died in his sleep that evening. Alcohol and methadone do not mix, as Peter well knew.

He'd been warned often enough by his physicians of the dangers of drinking while undergoing treatment for his heroin addiction. He'd ignored the warnings.

Both alcohol and methadone are depressants. The one will greatly enhance the sedative effects of the other. On top of that, most men who've abused alcohol for many years will have damaged their oesophagus, causing acid reflux, whereby the stomach reacts to the alcohol, often resulting in vomiting. Peter Comerford was drunk every day. If he'd been sick that evening in his sleep he could very easily have died – choking on his own vomit. He could also have died from too-shallow breathing, another effect of methadone that alcohol exacerbates.

As it was, he died not in his sleep but unusually violently. One likes to hope he was so "out of his mind" and sedated that he felt little of his final agony.

Caroline had decided to remain in the sitting-room and watch television, having no wish to join her drunken husband. She knew from bitter experience what he was capable of when in such a state – she had the scars to remind her.

Sure enough, barely two hours had elapsed before she heard Peter hollering for her. She ignored him.

"Come up here, you bitch!" he shouted again.

"No."

"Did you hear me? Would you fuckin' come up here."

Caroline switched off the television and stumbled into the hallway. "No!" she shouted. "I told you. I'm not coming up."

"I'm telling you, you bitch, come up here *now,* or I'll come down and get you."

A familiar pattern was being followed. Caroline knew where it would lead: a drunken quarrel over nothing, imagined slights and old bitterness trotted out, to culminate in a beating at her husband's hands.

"All right. I'm coming," she said wearily. Perhaps *this* time she could pacify him. If not, she'd fight her own corner, give as good as she got. She'd floored him a couple of times before, even putting him in the hospital. She was a powerfully built woman.

It was difficult negotiating the stairs in her inebriated state. She collided with the wall a couple of times before gaining the doorway of the bedroom.

She found a nude Peter lolling on the bed, one drunken hand grabbing at the air, beckoning her forward.

"Come over . . . come over here beside me!" he ordered.

"I fucking won't!"

"You fucking will!"

Despite his extreme intoxication Peter was on his feet within seconds. He seized her by the hair.

"You'll do as I say," he snarled.

She barely remembers what occurred next. There was a blazing row; Peter was out of control. He picked up a shoe and lashed out. She staggered back. He hit her again and again, the shoe smashing into her face. She could feel the blood spilling from her nostrils, the pain of her split lower lip. How many times had she suffered like this; how many more

86

"I can't forgive her," she says. "I can't believe what she did. How am I meant to forgive her? She's no daughter of mine! People keep telling me to go and see her but I'm sorry, I can't. How can I face her knowing what she did?"

Nor can Paul's children find it in their hearts to forgive their mother. Thus does greed destroy whole families.

The greed was ill-judged too. In the final analysis it emerged that the murderers had been playing for stakes that were considerably lower than they'd thought. Had the pair escaped justice then Jacqui stood to gain not the expected £300,000 but a sum closer to £90,000. This emerged after the PSNI's Financial Investigations Unit had looked into Paul's realizable assets. Of this lower sum Jacqui will see not a penny. It has been placed in a trust fund for the children's use.

8

THE MULHALL SISTERS
And the Tattletale Head

A Somalian called Farah Noor did not die an unusually violent death in Dublin on 20 March 2005. But a Kenyan named Sheilila Saïd Salim did. They were one and the same man.

Somalia has the unenviable distinction of topping the list of the world's most corrupt nations. Since 1994 the country has been torn by war and its people racked by famine. Had the international community not intervened in 2000 an estimated 300,000 might have starved to death.

Farah Noor, thirty-one, had arrived in Ireland in the winter of 1996 posing as a refugee fleeing the horrors of Somalia. He'd heard that Ireland was a land of drink, women and easy money for asylum-seekers. A land that held an irresistible attraction for the aimless hedonist. No matter that he had a wife and three children – aged seven, six and five – already missing him back in Mombasa,

Kenya. Ostensibly he was emigrating in search of work so that eventually they could join him. In reality Farah was off to have himself a party – a long and extended one.

Once he stepped out onto the tarmac at Dublin Airport that chilly morning, carrying nothing more than a change of clothing in a sports bag and a narcissistic determination in his heart, he had his sob story well prepared for the authorities.

En route he'd metamorphosed from Sheilila Saïd Salim to Farah Swaleh Noor and shaved two years from his real age. He was now from war-torn Mogadishu and had been languishing for the previous five years in a refugee camp. All his family had been slaughtered and he claimed he too would be killed if sent back to Somalia.

His story was credible. At least one million people had fled the country due to the calamitous war that had been raging there for nearly two decades; countless more were living in appalling conditions in refugee camps. The man who touched down at Dublin Airport in late 1996 claimed to have been among them.

In reality, however, Farah Noor – as he now called himself – was born in Mombasa; the only deceased member of his family was his father, a Somalian, who'd died when he, the asylum-seeker, was a boy. His mother is still very much alive and living in the Kenyan capital. As are his abandoned wife and children, of course. He has an older brother living in Toronto.

His first application for refugee status was rejected in 1997, but he appealed the decision and was finally allowed to live legally in Ireland in June 1999. Not that his uncertain immigrant status pre-1999 prevented Noor from doing as he pleased. From the moment of his arrival he wasted no time in acquainting himself with his "fellow" Somalians and investigating the many pubs and clubs in and around Dublin.

Alcohol was his passion – and would eventually be his undoing. He spent a great deal of his time drinking, often getting through several bottles of vodka a day, and taking drugs. He was violent by nature; he carried a Swiss army knife and a long dagger at all times. The alcohol only served to exacerbate his already volatile nature. He'd pick fights over imagined slights. A favoured ploy was to accuse others of making racist remarks before launching into an attack.

In August of 1997 he raped and impregnated a sixteen-year-old disabled Chinese girl, a virgin, in an amusement arcade on O'Connell Street. The girl – let us call her Sarah – would give birth to a baby boy whom Farah wanted nothing to do with. Later, during the trial of Linda and Charlotte Mulhall, the sisters accused of his murder, Sarah would testify to the violence and brutality she suffered at his hands.

Eight months following the rape Noor moved on to his next victim, another sixteen-year-old. Like all bullies he preyed on the naive and vulnerable. In contrast to his dalliance with "Sarah", his affair with "Mary" began tenderly: his natural charm quickly won her over. Before long she too became pregnant. Noor, according to Mary, was a model father and partner for three months following the birth, showering love and attention on her and their little son. But the "honeymoon" didn't last. Things would change when he rekindled his love affair with his demons, drugs and alcohol. Over the next two years he would rape and beat Mary almost every day.

The catalogue of horrors she suffered at his hands reads like the treatment for a sadistic porn movie. Too afraid to leave him lest he kill her, Mary endured the torture.

He controlled her every move. She was not permitted to leave the house, not even to visit the corner shop, without first asking permission. He allowed her to telephone no one, not even her family; he checked her mobile every night. He would accuse her of cheating on him – an impossibility, since she was effectively a prisoner. His insane accusations would be the prelude to yet another beating. On several occasions he stripped her naked, bound and blindfolded her, and forced her into adopting sick sexual poses, which he then captured with his camcorder. He took a fiendish delight in playing and replaying the videos, laughing as he freeze-framed image after image of the terrified girl, the girl who thought she loved him and who was the mother of his child. Any reluctance on her part was met with a beating. His word was iron-fisted law and he made sure she never lost sight of that.

A female lodger shared the house briefly with Noor and Mary. She moved out after three weeks – fearing that her life was in danger. Later she'd give an account of the brutality and sadism she witnessed.

"He'd beat Mary by slapping her across the face and knocking her to the ground," she recalled. "She'd curl up

123

on the ground to protect herself and he'd kick her. He would even do this when she was holding the baby. He'd no scruples whatsoever and when he was drunk he'd do this in front of anyone, both in public and back at the house. The main motivation for this was jealousy and possessiveness on Noor's behalf. There was never any reason for him to be this way but he would never believe her. It was like he was looking for an excuse to beat her."

With the help of the lodger and her parents, Mary finally escaped from Noor. He was having none of it; she'd wounded his pride. He stalked her relentlessly for almost a year after the split.

In 2001 Mary won full custody of their son. And in the summer of that same year Farah met Kathleen Mulhall.

Kathleen had been married twenty-nine years when she became involved with Farah Noor. They met at a Dublin nightclub – ironically being introduced through a friend of her eldest daughter Linda. One wonders what the mother of six grown-up children was doing nightclubbing with her daughter. But the Mulhalls were no ordinary family and they did not live by society's norms. They seemed to stumble about in a strange netherworld where having a "good time" took precedence over everything else.

On the surface, the attractive forty-five-year-old mother seemed an unlikely mate for the Kenyan, nine years her junior. She was more mature and more worldly-wise than his previous conquests. But there was obviously a need in Kathleen that could be exploited; perhaps she presented a feistier challenge. Whatever the reason on Noor's part, Kathleen fell under his spell and within a few months of meeting him had separated from her husband John.

Life for the Mulhalls had been rocky even before the Kenyan showed up, however. The Gardaí in Tallaght were kept well occupied with the family's activities. They attracted trouble like metal shards to a magnet and didn't seem capable of learning from their mistakes.

The Mulhall marriage had many fault lines running through it. Kathleen's husband, a casual worker for a glass company, was abusive towards his wife and had extramarital affairs. The two eldest sons James and John had racked up a sizable number of convictions between them and were serving prison sentences. Linda, the mother of four children, all under ten, led an aimless life, drinking and taking drugs, while her sister Charlotte funded an equally dissolute lifestyle through prostitution. But with the arrival of Farah Noor, the fractured lives of all these players would widen into a chasm that would eventually swallow them all.

Farah Noor was to ensure that their lives would never be the same again.

Bizarrely, when Kathleen announced the marriage was over she didn't fold her tent and quit the family home, as one might expect. Instead she moved her black boyfriend in, forcing her husband and children out. Naturally, such unorthodox behaviour didn't sit well with her friends and neighbours in Tallaght. With the antipathy towards the lovers growing, they chose to move to Cork.

Not surprisingly, the relationship between the pair was a stormy one. Over the next two years they lived at seven different addresses, getting by on benefits and spending most of their days drinking. Neighbours attested to being kept awake at night by their frequent brawls. Kathleen was often seen with bruising to her face; on several occasions she was hospitalized with bone fractures and damaged ribs. At one flat, the landlady saw splashes of blood on the walls of the hallway and living-room. She asked them to leave.

In between brutalizing Kathleen and going on his usual benders, Noor took odd jobs around the city to supplement his supplementary benefit. By 2004, whether they got fed up with Cork, or Cork got fed up with them, they moved back to Dublin. Back on the home turf, they lived at a succession of B&Bs and hotels, funded by social security. They were virtually nomads: their entire belongings fitted into a few sports bags, which they lugged from place to place.

Their final home was in Richmond Gardens, a run-down street in Ballybough, one of the poorer areas north of the Liffey. Croke Park is close by, as is the Royal Canal. They moved in on 1 December 2004. Farah Noor could not have imagined that 17 Richmond Gardens would be his last address on this earth, and that a mere three months later he would meet such a grisly end. Nor could he have imagined that members of the "fairer sex" he'd brutalized and tormented for most of his adulthood would be the architects of his death.

On her return to Dublin, Kathleen had set about rekindling her relationship with her family. The eldest daughter Linda and her sister Charlotte had been more forgiving of their mother's behaviour than other family members. Neither liked Farah. They resented this manipulative stranger who'd wrecked their parents' marriage – and who was beating and raping their mother. Yet they kept in touch and regularly visited the pair. That way they could keep an eye on Farah. Kathleen also made weekly visits to Wheatfield Prison, Clondalkin, to see her sons James and John Junior. But her husband and the two youngest children, Marie and Andrew, were not for turning. They were happy living with their father and refused to speak to her.

"A house divided against itself cannot stand," declared Abraham Lincoln in one of his most famous speeches. When the time came, the divisions in the Mulhall family would bring their house down, and Farah Noor with it.

On the morning of 20 March 2005, Charlotte and Linda Mulhall woke up in their Tallaght family home and wondered, as they did every morning, how to fill the long hours ahead. The following day would be Charlotte's twenty-second birthday. Charlotte – or Charlie as she preferred to be known – was looking forward to this particular birthday. Her twenty-first had failed to live up to the glorious coming-of-age celebration she'd been led to expect. In short, it had been a let-down. She was determined that this year things would be different. Better.

But no sooner had she thrown back the bed-covers on that bright spring morning than boredom set in, as it invariably did. Charlie had a foolproof way of offsetting it: vodka, and lots of it. Sunshine in a bottle. She reasoned that she might as well start her pre-birthday celebrations early.

She stumped to the kitchen, opened a fresh bottle and poured herself a generous glass. There was always a ready supply of alcohol in the Mulhall home, a commodity kept replenished with the same constancy as, say, tea or milk. so a vodka breakfast was by no means unusual for Charlie.

Drink and drugs had been staples in her life from the age of fifteen. Unemployed, on the dole, she'd turned to prostitution to fund her chaotic lifestyle and had even encouraged her mother to do a bit of job-sharing with her. They frequently worked the canal area off Baggot Street at weekends. Charlie was notorious among fellow-prostitutes for her pugnacity. No one dared encroach on her territory to try to take trade away from her. Tall and physically strong, she would let her fists do the talking. She claimed she could make as much as 2,500 for a "few good shags" and was a popular prostitute with men from the immigrant community. Charlotte got through many boyfriends, but given her temperament and her "profession", none of her liaisons lasted too long.

Prior to the slaying of Farah Noor she'd had many run-ins with the law, first coming to the attention of Gardaí when she was seventeen. By the eve of her twenty-second birthday the folder on Charlotte Mulhall had fattened considerably at Gardaí HQ, showing eleven arrests, fourteen charges and two convictions. She'd had few friends growing up and was devoted to her older sister Linda.

Thirty-one-year-old Linda was prettier and more sensitive than the combative Charlotte, but she led an equally purposeless life. Having suffered a number of violent relationships she'd resorted to self-harming, drugs and alcohol to numb the pain. She parted from the father of her children in 2000 and in 2003 took up with Wayne Kinsella.

Kinsella, a vicious thug, had notched up twenty-five convictions, including manslaughter and assault, before meeting Linda. Soon he started beating three of the children: her two boys aged ten and nine, and her eight-year-old daughter. He'd beat them with a belt and electrical flex, making them lie face down on beds in separate rooms, and going from room to room to mete out "punishment" until their little backs bled and he was out of breath.

Despite this cruelty, Linda remained besotted with the ruffian. It would take her a year to pluck up the courage to leave him. Eventually, largely through pressure from the authorities, she helped to have him prosecuted by testifying against him.

He received a seven-year prison sentence.

With Kinsella out of her life, Linda began drinking heavily and became increasingly dependent on drugs. The legacy of his abuse became too much to bear, and she made several suicide attempts. Her four children had been taken into care for the second time. That hurt: she loved her children and missed them dearly.

By that morning in March 2005, while Charlotte was pouring her first vodka of the day, Linda had managed to remain "clean" for several months. She'd regained custody of her children and was determined to keep it that way. She vowed not to lose them again.

"Linda, d'you want a glass?" asked Charlotte when Linda came into the kitchen in her night attire, still groggy from the previous night's imbibing.

"Naw, it's a bit early for me," said Linda, yawning.

"Oh, for fuck's sake! What's got into you? It's never too early for a vodka. There's fuck-all to do around here anyway. Here."

Charlotte poured her sister a generous tumbler of vodka and Coke.

"Well, maybe just the one."

"That's more like it," said Charlotte.

And with that the ladies retired to the sofa in the living-room to enjoy what would be the first of many glasses drunk on that fateful day. After a second vodka the world and life in general looked considerably brighter. To Charlotte at least.

Her mobile rang. It was their mother, calling to say that she and Farah were having a drink in the city centre.

Would the girls care to join them? Charlotte agreed with enthusiasm. She turned to Linda.

"Ma and Farah are having a drink in O'Connell Street. They want us to come down."

"No, I don't wanna go, Charlie. You go. I've got Sean to look after. I can't leave him on his own."

Linda's eleven-year-old son was upstairs, absorbed in a TV cartoon show.

But Charlotte wasn't going to take no for an answer. She poured her sister another drink; experience had taught her that Linda could often be swayed by a generous application of vodka.

"Come on Linda . . . please come. It'll be a bit of craic. Please."

"No, I don't think I can. I don't like Noor. I don't understand a bloody word he says."

"I know that, I don't like him either, but we don't have to talk to him. We'll just ignore him and talk to Ma . . . come on, Linda, *please*. It won't be the same if you don't come."

After ten more minutes, her resolve weakened by more and more vodka and tired of Charlotte's pestering, Linda finally gave in.

"All right," she sighed.

"Brilliant!" said Charlotte, jumping up. "Let's get our faces on then."

"But we have to take Sean. I'm not leaving him on his own."

Charlotte wasn't too keen on the notion. "For fuck's sake, Linda! How are we gonna get any decent drinking

131

done with your bloody brat yapping round after us? You're leaving him here. Sure isn't Andy here? He'll look after him."

Andrew, their youngest brother, was still asleep upstairs.

Linda brightened. She'd forgotten that Andrew was also in the house. Of course he'd look after young Sean for an hour or two.

Twenty minutes later, with the bottle of vodka finished and heavy make-up crookedly applied, the sisters made their way to the nearest bus stop to catch the number 77 into town.

They found their mother and Farah Noor outside McDonald's on O'Connell Street, swigging from cans of beer. Like Charlotte and Linda, they were already intoxicated. Drunkenness was a customary part of their daily routine. And like Charlotte and Linda, their basic needs already catered for by state benefits, Kathleen Mulhall and Farah Noor were free to live for the iniquitous pleasure of the moment, without a care in the world. They'd long since given up accountability for their actions and lost control of their own lives. Drug-fuelled, alcohol-addled days and nights had become the norm.

Farah was at the tail end of one of his by now infamous binges. He'd been drinking steadily for three days in the aftermath of the St Patrick's Day celebrations. It was not unusual for the Kenyan to get through three or four litre bottles of vodka a day – with a mad mélange of hard drugs as an accompaniment. Such an intake would doubtless be enough to fell the average man, but for Farah it was normal. His tolerance for alcohol was truly phenomenal.

The foursome wandered unsteadily about the city centre, wondering how to pass the time until darkness fell. All knew that more alcohol – that great alleviator of boredom – was the answer. But there was a problem: since all were on the dole they couldn't afford to go and sit in a pub. It would have to be a take-away.

With the decision made and Kathleen supporting Farah – now so far gone he could barely walk – they lurched in the direction of an off-licence on North Earl Street, where they bought a large bottle of vodka and four small bottles of Coke. Most of the cola was emptied out onto the pavement and the vodka passed around for the top-ups. Now they all could enjoy their "Coke" quite happily in public without fear of Garda interference. Public drinking is illegal in Dublin.

They repaired to benches down at the Liffey Boardwalk – an initiative of the city fathers intended as a courtesy to tourists but soon appropriated by the homeless and the addicted – and settled down to continue drinking.

Before leaving the house Linda had packed her supply of ecstasy tablets. There were ten in all and each had cost her 10. She seldom went anywhere without the drug. She took a tablet now and passed one to Charlotte. Their mother, not wishing to be left out, demanded one as well. But it was decided that Farah should not be given any. He was very drunk by this stage and, if past form was anything to go by, was liable to become aggressive at any time.

133

The day progressed pleasantly enough. The four continued drinking; Kathleen and her daughters each swallowed a further two tablets of ecstasy. But the demon in Farah was beginning to reveal itself, drugs or no drugs. He was becoming hostile, shouting and pulling at Kathleen for no good reason. Linda and Charlotte read the signs – and those signs were ominous. The sisters were well aware of Farah's violence towards their mother, and they knew that during his benders she suffered even more. It was getting late anyway: twilight was falling and rain was threatening. Charlotte told her mother she'd had enough; the party was over as far as she was concerned. She was going home.

The four drifted up O'Connell Street, Linda and Charlotte leading with Kathleen and the Kenyan staggering along behind. No love was being lost between the lovers: they were bawling and screaming at each other without a care for the scandalized onlookers. Farah had lapsed into an alcoholic haze; at one point he was so deluded that he grabbed at a little Chinese boy, believing it was his son. Kathleen managed to wrest the terrified youngster away from him.

Farah had dressed as he invariably did: jeans and one of his distinctive, long-sleeved Ireland "away" soccer jerseys. The squad was to play a qualifier in Tel Aviv in four days' time and Farah was excited at Ireland's prospects. But he was nevertheless among the few who wore that particular shirt. So distinctive was the design – white with a large Eircom logo – that a friend singled him out at once when the four returned to O'Connell Street. He was a fellow-African, Mohamed Ali Abubakar. The men exchanged pleasantries before going their separate ways.

Neither was to know that one of Dublin's ubiquitous CCTV cameras had captured their brief exchange. It had also recorded images of the three women who accompanied Farah that day.

Kathleen invited Linda and Charlie back to the flat she shared with Farah in Ballybough. They agreed; Charlie might yet have her birthday party. Her mood was improving by the hour, despite Farah's continued belligerence.

None owned a car – not that any of the four was in a fit state to drive. They could have taken the bus but decided against it. They arrived on foot in Richmond Gardens in early evening. The house looked deserted.

Once in the door of the flat, Kathleen produced the inevitable vodka and a mixer, and the drinking resumed. Somebody switched on the television set.

But Kathleen was a little concerned about Farah; he was making a nuisance of himself. She knew the very thing to calm him down. Before handing him his glass she crushed up Linda's last ecstasy tablet and slipped it into his vodka. The mixture had worked before and she believed it would work again.

It did not. Far from calming him it seemed to have the opposite effect. Farah was growing nasty again. He showed every sign of becoming a danger to whoever happened to be in his vicinity. And of the three women Linda was within groping distance. His libidinous eye fell upon her.

Linda Mulhall, the eldest of the family, is by anyone's standards an attractive woman: slim of build, with long fair hair and a pretty face. She bears a striking resemblance to her mother – a younger version as it were. That day, despite her inebriated state – and despite an inflammation to her upper lip brought on by a decorative stud – she'd have appeared irresistible to the womanizing Farah. He sat down beside her on the settee. Without any preamble he began touching her sexually.

Linda was disgusted. She tried to repel his advances, being conscious that her mother in particular would not be pleased. But he would not desist. Although no more than five feet six inches tall, he was a muscular, well-built individual. Many an opponent in a pub brawl had misjudged Farah's strength. No matter how much she struggled, Linda could not extricate herself from his grip. He grew increasingly amorous.

Kathleen and Charlotte continued to watch television, pretending not to notice and hoping Farah would simply give up in the face of Linda's opposition. They knew that it took very little "to set him off", so for now it was best to humour him.

But the Kenyan was not so easily discouraged. He locked his arms about Linda's waist and refused to let go. She began to panic. She struggled to her feet with difficulty. Farah held on tight and rose also. There was no way to shake him off.

Kathleen could ignore him no longer. She screamed abuse at him, as did Charlotte. But Farah just smirked and made a cutting gesture with his finger across his throat. He'd threatened to kill Kathleen countless times and this was his way of telling her that she'd better keep quiet or she'd be sorry.

"We're two creatures of the night, you and me," he whispered in Linda's ear. "You're just like your mother."

"What the fuck are you saying to her, Farah?" Kathleen hollered. "Get your bloody hands off her."

Linda managed to stumble down to the kitchen. She was wailing now, still trying to work herself loose from Farah's grip, but he clung on doggedly. She flailed at his hands, wrists; she could not budge him. It was as if he was made of steel. He was determined to have his way with her. All sense of decency and propriety had deserted him. He was oblivious to Kathleen's roars and threats.

Charlotte, ever the loyal sister, rushed to Linda's aid and tried to free her.

"Get your fucking hands off her, Farah!" she screamed. "Get your fucking hands off her *now*!"

Charlotte was a lot stronger than her mother and sister. But although she could well fight her corner on the grim streets of the red-light district, she was no match for the Kenyan. It was as if his arms were bolted onto Linda.

Something happened in the following moments, however, to change Farah's mind. Much to Linda's relief, he let her go. He'd had another idea. He turned abruptly, grabbed Kathleen and began pushing her towards the bedroom, repeating the throat-cutting gesture he'd made earlier. If he couldn't have the daughter, the mother would have to do.

"Kill him for me!" Kathleen pleaded of her girls as she was manhandled roughly. "Please kill him for me."

Charlotte needed no more coaxing. Knowing what she already knew about Farah, and given the hyperactive state she was in, she went to the kitchen and returned with a Stanley knife. In the wrong hands it's a fearsome weapon: when fresh, one of its disposable blades can be as sharp as a surgeon's scalpel.

Farah anticipated no opposition to his abuse of Kathleen – or any other woman. He'd met with none before. From the time of his arrival in Ireland six years before he'd been able to have his way with every woman he took a shine to, young and old. The last thing he expected was that the mouse would eventually roar.

And roar it did that night. Howling like a creature demented, Charlotte attacked Farah from behind. With her left hand she yanked his head back.

With one deft stroke she slit his throat with the knife in her right.

The gash was deep. Blood spurted forth from the severed arteries, spraying the walls, spattering over Kathleen.

"Get him away from me!" Kathleen screamed upon realizing what had happened. "For God's sake get him away from me!"

The dying man stumbled over the threshold and into the bedroom. He fell heavily against the bed. Somehow he managed to raise himself, briefly.

"Kathy!" he moaned, clutching at his throat. "Oh, Kathy!"

Those were his last words.

Charlotte lunged at him a second time with the knife. Linda, meanwhile, had grabbed a hammer from the kitchen and hurried now to aid her sister. She brought the hammer down on Farah's head. Hard. She heard his skull crack.

Fearing he might still be alive, the two redoubled the attack in a savage frenzy. Linda struck Farah countless times with the hammer. Charlotte was stabbing at every part of his anatomy. Soon the white football shirt had turned crimson.

Their mother, meanwhile, had returned to the living-room. She sat quietly, drinking her vodka and Coke and feigning interest in a TV programme, while trying to block out the sounds of slaughter emanating from the bedroom. She could not have helped hearing the commotion; the bedroom was no more than a dozen feet away from where she was sitting. She could not have helped hearing Farah's final howls of agony as he was slaughtered like a pig. But such was the hatred she'd developed for the man she'd once professed to love that she did not even look in upon the scene of butchery.

Or she was afraid to – afraid that it would all prove too much for her.

Her daughters stopped at last, each breathing heavily, tears streaming down their cheeks. They could hardly believe what they'd done. The ruined body of Farah Noor lay sprawled in a darkening mess of blood that was spreading out across the carpet like some ghastly ink-blot test. The walls – even the ceiling – of the small bedroom were spattered. Blood had drenched Charlotte and Linda's bodies, saturating their clothing.

They knelt over the corpse, each staring hard at the other, unable to say a word. It was unreal, surreal. Such things didn't happen in the real world – not in *their* world at any rate. People stole, got into fights, did bad things. But no one killed a man as if his body were a hunk of meat with a head and limbs attached. It was brutal and they were appalled. *They* had done it.

"He's dead," Charlotte said at last. "He's dead."

Linda nodded unhappily. Stunned, they fell into each other's bloodied arms and wept.

Kathleen Mulhall still sat expressionless in front of the TV. Her glass was empty.

She heard movement, and turned. Her daughters were emerging from the place of slaughter, each clutching a blood-smeared weapon in a grotesque parody of *Macbeth*'s après-murder scene.

"We're after killing him, Ma," Charlotte said simply.

Kathleen stared in stupefaction at their drenched clothing; at the trail of Farah's blood they'd tracked in from the bedroom. It was too much for her; she broke down, by turns weeping and screaming hysterically. The daughters took up the cry. The three held onto one another. The physical contact was lending them some kind of comfort and strength amid the horror.

How long they remained thus is impossible to know: ecstasy pills have a way of telescoping one's perception of the passage of time. But eventually the tears were all shed, the emotions spent; reality was kicking in. Kathleen was the first to speak; she'd recovered. The enormity of the killing had sunk in. Now she was fearful.

"Get him out of here!" she ordered. "You must get him out."

That gave the sisters pause. In keeping with the thoughts and fears of all first-time killers before them, the Mulhall sisters asked themselves how they were going to do that. How would they – or could they – dispose of Farah Noor's corpse?

The healthy human body when living is a miracle of motion and adaptability. It's lithe and amazingly portable – that is, when its owner is doing the porting. But a dead body is an entirely different matter. It's an awkward, cumbersome mass of bone and tissue. It's no coincidence that we speak of something being a "dead weight". Corpses are heavy and ample. They are not disposed of easily.

Picture the scene. Two inebriated young women have frenetically slashed a man to death. They gaze down in dismay at the earthly remains of Farah Noor who, just minutes before, had been quick and dangerous. Now he's no more than a lifeless collection of organic matter.

That collection must be disposed of – removed from the house where their mother lives, lest she be incriminated in the murder.

Given the huge amount of alcohol each had consumed that day it's extremely doubtful that Kathleen and her daughters were in their "right mind". Add to this the number of ecstasy tablets that were playing merry hell with their synapses and it becomes clear that none of the three was capable of making a rational decision.

They could have gone to the authorities, confessed the crime and thrown themselves upon the mercy of the courts. Linda had most to lose: a prison sentence would undoubtedly have meant parting from her four children. She might never see them again. She'd lost them before.

Linda and Charlotte Mulhall were incapable of coherent thought, unable to make decisions that would leave them and their mother in the clear. In simple terms, they were criminals. They had killed; there was a dead body in a flat rented in their mother's name. It had to be disposed of.

Farah's corpse must be taken elsewhere. A number of possibilities presented themselves. They could take the body to a distant location, as far away as possible from the scene of the crime, and bury it. But since none of them owned a car this option was a non-starter. They could conceal it in the apartment or in another part of the building. But corpses by their nature tend to disintegrate, to decompose, to stink after a time.

There was no argument: Farah's remains would have to be moved elsewhere.

We do not know whose idea it was to carve up the corpse. Linda insisted it was Charlotte's idea and Charlotte said it was their mother's. What we do know is that it was the sisters who engaged in the dreadful operation. They would later claim that their mother had no hand in either the killing or dismembering. There is no reason to doubt their insistence.

They dragged Farah's corpse into the en-suite bathroom. The bathroom, in keeping with the rest of the flat, was filthy. Perhaps the previous tenant had cleaned it at one time. Kathleen and Farah had not. The tiled walls and floor were coated with a layer of dirt; hairs and other human detritus lay everywhere. Every square inch of the shower cubicle was grimy and sticky to the touch.

The sisters pushed and pulled, attempting to force the body of the dead African into the tiny cubicle. It was not built to accommodate a prone, five-foot-six man. Farah's head protruded into the bathroom.

In order to carve up a corpse you need a saw or a hatchet. Without such tools to hand they had to improvise. Linda found a bread knife in the kitchen to supplement Charlotte's Stanley knife and the hammer. Thus equipped, they set about the butchery.

Linda sat on the toilet seat covering her face while Charlotte took control of things. She pulled off Farah's jeans. Her intention was to amputate his left leg above the knee. The Stanley knife was still sharp. She set to severing the leg. Linda wept as she heard the blade grind against bone, and slice through tendon and muscle. It was strenuous work, but the ecstasy tablets and the alcohol had released in Charlotte an uncharacteristic energy and strength. Sweating now, she threw down the knife and picked up the hammer, smashing it again and again into the kneecap as Linda looked on through latticed fingers. Finally, with the bone shattered and the cartilage "tenderized", a few more slicing actions with the bread knife were all that was required. The lower leg came free. Linda fetched a roll of bin-liners and handed one to Charlotte, who bagged up the leg and put it to one side.

Emboldened now by her sister's quick mastery of coarse dissection, Linda took up the hammer and proceeded to smash it into the right leg. Time after time after time. She delivered as many blows as she could until exhaustion set in and she had to sit back on the toilet seat to regain her strength. Charlotte showed no such weakness, however. She was already sawing into the second kneecap, using the same method as before.

There was blood everywhere as litre by litre it ebbed away from the terrible dismemberment in progress. Linda fetched towels to try and soak it up.

With the second leg severed and stowed away the women laboured diligently over the corpse for the next four or more hours: severing the arms, the thighs below the hip bone, hammering and sawing, pausing only to wipe the sweat and blood from their brows; the strands of matted hair that would insist on falling across their eyes. It was excruciatingly hard work; Farah Noor had been a strong man. The knives soon blunted on the resilient muscles and sinews built up over a lifetime of brawling and weight-training. Often the sisters had to resort to the hammer, pounding away at tissue and bone to make it less resistant to blades that were growing ever blunter.

"It took us a few hours to do it," Linda would set down in a statement to the Gardaí. "Me ma did not cut him up. We had to put a towel over there when we were removing his legs to stop the blood rushing out. We cut him on the knees and on the elbows. Me ma had told me already that he'd raped her and I said, 'He won't rape my ma again.' I cut his private parts off. The long piece, not the balls. We threw it in the canal with the rest."

"It" would never be recovered.

Finally all that remained attached to the torso was the head itself.

Linda couldn't bear to look upon Farah's face. His fixed, staring eyes disturbed her. She covered the head with a towel before they each took part in the grisly task of decapitation.

It was, arguably, the most distasteful and unsettling phase of the mutilation. Yet it proved to be the easiest: Charlotte's initial "work" with the Stanley knife had begun the job of beheading. She need only widen and deepen the wound she'd made in the throat and neck. Then they were sawing and hacking at the place where the spinal cord joins the base of the skull. A few more deft blows and the towel-covered head fell away.

The macabre deed completed, the sisters joined their mother in the living-room. They were worn out from their exertion. The effects of the ecstasy and alcohol were lessening and the horrific realization of what they'd just done began to truly dawn on them. They stood facing each other in the little room, by turns sobbing and cursing.

More drink was needed. Kathleen poured fresh glasses of neat vodka as a new set of problems presented itself.

The bathroom resembled a chamber of horrors. It would have to be cleaned. The body parts would have to be disposed of, and the disposal must take place before daylight. The head would have to be consigned to a separate place. How would they transport the remains from the scene of the crime?

As the vodka imbued them with fresh reserves of Dutch courage, the Mulhall women discussed the very real possibility of somebody noticing Farah's absence. On the plus side Farah had no relatives in Ireland, so he wouldn't be missed for some time. If the Guards came asking, they'd say he'd taken off with another woman. He was known far and wide as a womanizer, therefore it was a highly plausible story. It meant of course that *all* traces of him would have to be removed from the flat, his clothes and personal effects included. The bedding and carpet would also have to go. The evidence of his life and death was everywhere. Although the old Hollywood gangsters often spoke of "rubbing out" an enemy, the Mulhalls were beginning to appreciate that it wasn't quite as simple as it sounded.

They would need help. There was only one person they could call on: John Mulhall, the girls' father. Linda telephoned him at around midnight.

John did not know what to make of the call. Linda was clearly very distressed. She gave him to understand that something dreadful had happened. He thought initially that she and her sister had overdosed on some substance or other – or were just plain drunk. They were at their mother's flat, he learned. He had no great desire to go there, to have to speak to the woman who'd walked out on him three years earlier. Nor to meet the foreign thug who'd brought so much heartache into his family.

"We need you, Da," Linda pleaded. "Me ma needs you as well."

Charlotte took the phone and spoke to her father. Her pleading was equally earnest. Something was definitely up, John concluded. The girls were out of their minds with worry; he'd seldom heard them so upset.

"Put your ma on," he said.

Kathleen convinced him. He climbed into his van and went to investigate. Linda admitted him. The others were in the living-room; he noted that all three had tear-stained faces and smudged mascara. He also noted the spatters of blood on his daughters' faces and clothing. He looked furtively about him.

"What's going on?" he asked. "Where's Farah?"

Charlotte was the first to speak. "He's in the hall, Da."

Puzzled, John put his head around the door and looked up and down the hallway. There was no sign of Farah. "What are you saying? There's no one there."

The women stared at John Mulhall, wondering how to express the unspeakable.

"What the hell's going on? Where *is* he?"

Linda and Kathleen turned away, leaving Charlotte to explain.

"He's in the bags, Da," she said at last, staring at the floor.

"*What!*"

Not quite believing what he'd heard, her father untied one of the bin-bags and had a peek inside.

"Oh, Jesus Christ!" he yelled out, recoiling from the horror. "Oh my God!"

"He was gonna rape Linda, Da. He was gonna kill our ma."

"I don't care what he was gonna do! You're on your own now. I'm having no part of this." With that, John Mulhall left the flat hurriedly without a backward glance.

The sisters felt betrayed. They couldn't believe he'd desert them in their hour of desperation. By then they were exhausted, both mentally and physically. They collapsed into bed, weeping uncontrollably, and tried to sleep for a few hours.

But later that night John had a change of heart. At six in the morning he returned to the flat. He told his estranged wife and daughters that he'd help with the bloodstained bed-linen and other items that could incriminate them; he'd store them in the family home in Tallaght and get rid of them in due course. Good as his word, he filled several bin-liners.

The mortal remains of Farah Noor, however, he'd leave to the women to dispose of. They killed him; he was their responsibility.

Her father having departed for the second time, Charlotte took control. The body parts, she decided, could *not* be carried on a bus. The smells would arouse suspicion – for it is a distasteful fact that upon death the body releases its waste matter. They would stuff the parts into sports bags and carry them down to the Royal Canal, a short distance from the flat. Ballybough's early risers were already going about their business; three women making trips to the canal would not go unremarked. Instead they'd wait until the morning rush hour. There was safety in numbers.

By 7 a.m. the Mulhall women, more at ease now that their father was on their side, had washed and tidied themselves up. The trio set out on the first of several grim expeditions.

They walked the short distance to the Royal Canal. Nothing about them appeared out of the ordinary as they trudged along, blending in, as they did, with scores of reluctant commuters on their way to work. The sisters carried the macabre cargo in two sports bags. Linda lugged Farah's arms in the bag at her side and Charlotte had the much heavier torso slung from her shoulders. Kathleen didn't carry anything, she being the chief mourner in this very unusual funeral cortege. Her duty was to keep watch as her daughters hauled out the heavy bin-liners and committed her lover's ruined corpse to the murky water.

It was at this stage – the disposal of the remains – that the women revealed a stunning lack of common sense.

They chose a canal instead of a river. The static canal water ensured that the body parts would not be carried away, to end up out in Dublin Bay. Nor did they consider where the deepest areas might lie. As ill-luck would have it, they dropped the body parts into one of the shallowest stretches of water.

In all they made five trips back and forth between the flat and the canal, emptying and refilling the sports bags, until they'd dumped the eight pieces of Farah.

Once back at the crime scene they continued with the cleaning. They did a thorough job – for women who were not used to living in tidy surroundings. In their efforts that day to eradicate all traces of the murder, they soon depleted the shelf of cleaning agents at their local supermarket. When they were done the bedroom was as new and the bathroom sparkled.

The last problem was Farah's head. It still reposed in a bin-bag in the hallway. It was the weakest link in their chain of disposal: the head was recognizable, undeniably that of Farah Noor. It would have to be spirited away to a faraway destination. In the collective Mulhall mind, "far away" meant the far side of town. They accordingly devised a plan to travel by bus across the city and bury the head in Tymon Park, an amenity area in Ballyboden on the periphery of Dublin South.

They decided not to use the sports bags from the earlier mission. They had leaked and were beginning to reek of death, a problem that could only get worse in a warm bus. But Kathleen produced a camera bag. She reckoned it was just about big enough for the purpose: it fitted Farah's head snugly.

They left the flat at noon. They were peckish, though, and voted to have something to eat before boarding the bus. One wonders how the trio could think about food in the circumstances, but obviously they weren't so squeamish. Besides, more than twenty-four hours had passed since they'd last eaten. CCTV footage shows them queuing at the deli counter in a minimarket and ordering two fried breakfasts and a salad roll. Linda has the camera bag with its gruesome contents strapped to her back.

On reaching Tymon Park they couldn't decide where to bury the head and wandered around for hours trying to find a suitable spot. Finally during a cigarette break on one of the park benches, Charlotte, anxious to get the deed done, began to claw at the earth with her bare fingers. The ground was hard and the resulting hole was shallow, but it would have to do. She removed the head from the bag while the others averted their eyes, dumped it without ceremony into the hole and kicked the dirt back over it.

By then it was approaching seven thirty. It had been a very long day. Charlotte stared down wanly at the trampled earth, at the makeshift grave containing Farah's head. All at once she remembered what day it was: 21 March – her birthday. The birthday she'd hoped would be less boring than her twenty-first was certainly proving to be otherwise.

It had turned into a nightmare.

The Mulhall women might have rid themselves physically of Farah Noor, but mentally he was still very much alive. Linda, the most sensitive of the three, could not cope in the aftermath of the murder. She couldn't sleep. The dead man's head would swim into her vision and start speaking to her as soon as she shut her eyes. Even when fully awake she'd see him in the darkness of the bedroom and in every mirror she looked in. Her mind was in turmoil. She started to drink heavily to try and block out the memories, but nothing worked. In her deluded state, she felt there was only one way to end the torment: exhume Farah's head from Tymon Park and destroy it. She'd ask her mother to help her.

On 30 March, ten days following the murder, Linda decided to look in on her mother. Upon reaching Ballybough on foot, she was dismayed to see a commotion on the bridge overlooking the Royal Canal. A group of bystanders had gathered and were talking excitedly. Several Guards were present. Her heart sank to her boots. She *knew* immediately that the body parts had surfaced. She kept her head down and hurried on her way.

Kathleen was panic-stricken on hearing the news. Mother and daughter sat on the sofa, clutching each other and weeping. They wondered what to do. They simply had to know the truth, even if their hearts already told them that the canal had yielded up its secret. The old adage holds true: the murderer always returns to the scene of the crime. They pulled on their coats and headed down to the bridge. A flurry of activity – uniformed Gardaí and men in white forensic overalls at the place they'd dumped the remains – confirmed their worst fears.

From that moment on, the Mulhall women rarely missed a news broadcast. Those were nail-biting days. And yet, as long as the Gardaí were unable to identify the dismembered corpse, they were relatively safe. The head was the key: the head that haunted Linda's dreams and even intruded into her waking hours. It was more important than ever to retrieve it and destroy it.

After sleepless nights and days of heavy drinking she summoned up the courage to carry out the distasteful operation. She returned to Tymon Park and disinterred the head. Back home, she rang Kathleen.

"I'm after digging up Farah's head," she told her. "I have it here in a bag, Ma. You'll have to help me get rid of the thing for good."

But her mother wanted no part of it. Linda was on her own.

Linda was both angry and upset. She went to the kitchen and returned with a bottle of vodka and a hammer. Having emptied out the contents of a child's schoolbag, she stuffed the decomposing head into it, along with the hammer and vodka. Thus prepared, she set out in the early hours on a forty-minute walk that would take her to Killinarden Hill – an area close to the Mulhall family home in Tallaght.

It was a misty, grey morning and there were no witnesses to what she was about to do. She recalls only black birds that seemed somehow ominous to her as they cawed eerily in the treetops. Later she'd give a full account of her expedition to detectives.

"I walked into a far field and kissed the bag and told Farah I was sorry. I stayed there for ages, a long time. I had a bottle of vodka with me. I drank all of it. I took the hammer out of the bag. I left the head in the bag and hit it loads of times to break it up. I fell asleep and woke up cold. It was starting to get dark. There was a mucky patch there and I turned away and pulled the head out of the bag. I put muck over it and said a prayer and told him I was sorry and said it should not be you, it should be me ma. I burned the plastic bag up there and the schoolbag. And I ran home to bed. I am sorry for what happened. It is not my fault it happened. I'm sorry. If I could turn back time I would. I am sorry."

But this confession would come much later. In the meantime Charlotte and Kathleen seemed to be coping better than Linda. That, at least, could be inferred from their actions in the wake of the murder. Just days after Farah's death the pair began using his debit card to withdraw money from his account. Charlotte sold his gold chain and rings to junkies on the streets. She also passed his mobile phone to her father, who sold it for 50 to a work colleague.

Charlotte and Kathleen took off to Manchester for a week, a trip Linda had planned for early April. Initially both daughters were to have accompanied their mother. The reason for the trip? Linda was to have an abortion; four children were enough for her. But the "pregnancy" turned out to be a false alarm. Nevertheless, her mother and sister had their hearts set on the little break – and heaven knows but they needed it more than ever now. They went without Linda.

The pair spent ten days in England, staying in hostels for the homeless, sleeping rough on park benches, and doing some serious drinking. So much that funds soon ran low. Not to worry, though: in the course of an evening's carousing Charlotte hooked up with a gentleman who took care of expenses, and they spent the best part of a week sharing his hotel room.

Soon, however, they tired of Manchester and wished to return home. But there was a snag: the cost of the ferry. Again Charlotte saved the day: she rang the Irish social services, who furnished them with tickets. They could rejoin Linda and await developments.

Following the recovery of the body parts, Gardaí spent a month trying to discover the identity of the man in the canal. They drew a blank. They trawled through countless hours of CCTV footage and spoke to members of the immigrant community. They even considered the possibility that they might be dealing with a ritual sacrifice killing, or *muti*, still practised in certain parts of Africa.

The breakthrough came on 9 May. Bus-driver Mohamed Ali Abubakar was leafing through a copy of *Metro*

Éireann, the multicultural tabloid, when his eye fell upon a public-service announcement. The police were appealing for information on the identity of the dismembered man found in the canal. Ali immediately recognized the photo of the white Ireland-away football jersey. His friend Farah Noor had been wearing one similar the last time he'd seen him on O'Connell Street back on 20 March. He'd been trying to contact Farah for weeks, but his friend's mobile was switched off. Ali feared the worst and reported his suspicions to Gardaí. He'd socialized on occasion with Farah and Kathleen and was acquainted with the Mulhall sisters. He told Gardaí about his last sighting of the three women, when they'd been accompanying Farah in the city centre.

With a possible name to go with the torso and severed limbs, detectives began looking into Farah Swaleh Noor's background. They interviewed his former partner Mary and took a saliva swab from her baby son for DNA matching. They visited Noor's last known address, Flat 1 at Ballybough, and spoke to Kathleen. Kathleen had now moved into flat number four in the same house; she was sharing it with a young Russian who spoke no English. Yes, she'd had a relationship with Farah Noor, but he'd run off with an ex-girlfriend and she hadn't seen him "in ages".

The detectives focused their investigation on Flat 1. They noted that parts of the carpet had been removed and replaced with newer patches. They took swab samples from the furniture and walls, to be subjected to forensic analysis.

But it would be six weeks before the DNA results were made available.

Meanwhile, Noor's bank records showed that his last transaction was made on 30 March, the day the body parts were recovered. Clearly someone else was using his card. With the help of Vodafone they determined his mobile number and traced its activity. The man found to be in possession of the phone was a colleague of John Mulhall . . .

At the time of the murder and in its aftermath, the elder Mulhall boys, James and John junior, were serving prison sentences: one for dangerous driving causing death, the other for car theft. They were well known to police, having notched up twenty-three convictions between them. John junior was a heavy heroin user.

Their mother and sisters Linda and Charlotte were frequent visitors to the prison during the months following the murder. Linda was particularly close to James. At some point between April and July, with the weight of their crime weighing heavily upon them, the women confessed their dreadful deeds to the boys. It seemed the thing to do: a problem shared. They could not know that their confiding in their nearest and dearest would serve to unravel everything, like a loose thread in cheap cotton. It's said that there's no honour among thieves. By extension, that would prove true of the Mulhalls, a family not known for its lofty morality.

On 11 July Garda Damien Duffy received a very unusual phone call. It was from John Mulhall junior. He

157

had information on the body in the canal. He could, he claimed, name names: that of the victim *and* of those who'd carried out his murder.

The following day Gardaí interviewed John and James in Wheatfield Prison. The pair told them the full story as it had been related to them by Kathleen back in April. They confirmed that Linda and Charlotte had also confided in them, and had corroborated all their mother had said. Farah and Kathleen had been lovers, they said; on the night of 20 March in Flat 1, Richmond Gardens, Farah had made a pass at Linda, as a result of which the girls, urged on by their mother, were forced to kill him before he grew too violent.

According to the boys, their mother was to blame for the murder. She'd got their sisters drunk, had plied them with drugs so that they'd carry out the killing for her. They described the dismembering and dumping of the body parts, how their father helped ferry away the bed covers. They attested to the excessive cleaning of the flat and the crude redecoration: their mother had assembled ill-matching pieces of rug to replace the bloodstained areas of carpet.

The police investigation had been moving with glacial velocity for three months. Suddenly the case was opening up with a speed that surprised the detectives. On the very day of the brothers' confession, the Science Lab reported that the DNA sample taken from Mary's son matched that of the torso. The Lab also confirmed that the swabs taken in the Ballybough flat contained DNA belonging to Farah Noor.

Detectives now had enough evidence to arrest the Mulhalls.

They swooped on all four – John senior, Kathleen, Linda and Charlotte – simultaneously at ten in the morning on 3 August. They were held at separate locations for the interrogations. But in the teeth of such strong evidence all denied involvement in the murder. It might be thought the authorities had assembled enough proof to prefer charges there and then. But the evidence was circumstantial; Gardaí were looking for an admission of guilt from at least one of the suspects. Yet after twelve hours of questioning none was forthcoming; the Guards had no choice but to release all four.

Of the three women, Linda seemed to Gardaí to be the most susceptible to sustained pressure. They felt sure she would crack over time.

Upon their release from custody, the Mulhall women went their separate ways. Each did her best to live with the burden of their horrendous act. Kathleen cut off all contact with her daughters. Charlotte disappeared back to her life of prostitution. Linda moved into the family home in Tallaght, there to join her father and young sister Marie. Unable to sleep, drinking heavily and neglecting her children, she came under sustained pressure from her father and sister to come clean to the Gardaí. Such was the pressure they exerted on her, coupled with her guilty conscience, that Linda attempted suicide. She slashed her wrists.

She finally caved in and agreed to speak to the Guards again. Sixteen days had passed since she, Kathleen and Charlotte had parted company. She made a full verbal and written statement detailing the events of 20 and 21 March, and incriminating the others. When finished she agreed to accompany two detectives to Killinarden Hill to show them where she'd buried the head.

It would prove to be a fruitless effort. Despite that first search and subsequent searches by teams of Gardaí, Farah's head was never recovered. Police suspect that it may have been carried away by a wild animal, perhaps a fox or a badger.

On 14 September Linda was charged with Farah Noor's murder.

Kathleen Mulhall, having got wind of her daughter's confession, had fled to Carlow. She was arrested there on the day Linda was charged and brought back to Dublin for questioning. Despite Linda's testimony, Kathleen claimed to know nothing about the murder. She would have the detectives believe that Linda was a mentally disturbed girl, who used drugs and was bulimic.

"It relates to her dad," Kathleen stated. "If she wants to talk to you about it she can, but it's not my business."

She said that living with Farah Noor had been "hell" and gave an account of the innumerable assaults she'd suffered: "broken ribs, two fractured hands and head injuries". His brutality had resulted in her being hospitalized at least three times.

"He'd beat me with his hands, his fists or his belt. He'd mostly use a belt. He told me on a number of occasions that if I told anyone about the attacks he would kill me. I believed him when he said this. I'm one hundred per cent sure he was telling the truth when he said he'd kill me. That's why I got away from him."

She attested to the fact that he regularly self-harmed by burning himself with cigarettes.

"He'd put the lit cigarette to various parts of his body and just let the skin burn," she claimed. "About five or six times I woke up with cigarette burns. I'd have been drinking and in a deep sleep and the following morning I'd see the burn marks."

Kathleen broke down several times during the interview. Notwithstanding all the violence she'd suffered at his hands she was sorry he was dead – or so she claimed. But she was adamant that she had no part in his death. He'd left her for another woman and that was all she knew. Linda could say what she liked; Kathleen was innocent.

With no real evidence to convict her, the Gardaí had to let Kathleen go.

Having secured Linda's confession, detectives moved in on Charlotte. They enlisted the help of her father, John Mulhall. He'd helped them to persuade Linda to talk. Would he help them again? Eventually he agreed.

But Charlotte was made of sterner stuff. She claimed that her mother had murdered Farah. She and Linda had visited her that evening to find the flat "covered in blood". The detectives persisted, and after five hours of grilling she gave in.

On 17 October, nearly eight months after his death, Charlotte was charged with Farah Noor's murder.

With his daughters in custody for a crime that remained a talking point in pubs across Dublin and beyond, John Mulhall found life very difficult indeed. He wept every time he saw his daughters' faces on the television. He had helped in eliciting their confessions, but doing the right thing had brought him little comfort. Two sons of his were in prison and now two daughters would be going behind bars for life.

He had failed his family.

In the early hours of 8 December, nine months following the murder, and ten months before his daughters would stand trial, the fifty-three-year-old father drove to Phoenix Park and hanged himself.

The nine-day trial of Linda and Charlotte, which commenced on 12 October 2006, was the most lurid and sensational ever heard in an Irish court. Justice Paul Carney presided; six men and six women made up the jury. It would take them a total of eighteen hours to decide their verdicts.

Charlotte Mulhall was found guilty of murder by a ten-to-two majority. An eleven-to-one majority returned a verdict of manslaughter on Linda Mulhall.

The sisters wept openly as they were led away. They were hugged by their traitorous brothers, James and John.

The pair, freed from prison, had followed the proceedings from the public gallery.

Six weeks later Charlotte and Linda were back in court to hear their sentences. Judge Carney opened proceedings by stating that the Farah Swaleh Noor murder was "the most grotesque case of killing" that he'd ever had to deal with. It was the third case of its kind, a murder involving mutilation, to make Irish legal history. Older readers will recall Shan Mohangi, a South African medical student who killed Hazel Mullen in 1963. He dismembered the corpse. Having served only three years in jail he was deported back to South Africa, where he changed his name and went into politics. In 1996 Dubliner Michael Bambrick was sentenced to eighteen years for the murder of two women, Patricia McCauley and Mary Cummins. Like Mohangi and the Mulhalls he'd cut up the bodies, and buried the parts near his home.

Justice Carney lost no time in sentencing the pair before him. Linda received fourteen years. He gave Charlotte the mandatory sentence of life behind bars.

Kathleen Mulhall was conspicuously absent from the trial of her daughters. She'd fled to live with her brother in Birmingham in October 2006 and did not return to Ireland until February 2008.

She was arrested and charged with helping to clean up the murder scene, withholding information and giving false information. In February 2009 she pleaded guilty to concealing evidence relating to Farah's murder and was due to be sentenced at the time of goint to print.

163

Two months following the close of the sisters' trial another family member was before the courts. James Mulhall, aged thirty-five, having completed his three-year sentence for causing death by dangerous driving, was being tried together with an accomplice for robbing two prostitutes. His defence plea – that he was caring for Linda's four children, along with six of his own and he therefore needed the money – was dismissed by the judge. He found Mulhall guilty of assault and theft and handed down a five-year sentence. Bizarrely, James had taken advantage of breaks during the trial of his sisters to steal 1000 and nine mobile phones from the prostitutes.

In March 2008 Charlotte Mulhall lost an appeal against her conviction. In April of the same year Linda Mulhall appealed against the severity of her sentence on the grounds that the trial judge was not shown her probation and psychological reports before passing sentence. She too lost her appeal. The Court of Criminal Appeal decided that the gruesome nature of the crime meant that her fourteen-year sentence was appropriate and should be at the "very, very serious end of the scale".

In January 2009 Linda made a second appeal. At the time of writing, it was still going through the courts.

9

UNA BLACK
The Neighbour, the Puppy and the Murder

In 1986 a Galwayman sexually abused a little girl of six. No charges were ever brought against him. He went on with his life, oblivious to the consequences of his action. He was not to know that it would result indirectly in the death of an innocent man twenty years later, the imprisonment of that man's killer, and the depriving of a baby boy of his mother's loving care.

That little girl was Una Black. In the wake of the sexual abuse, her life descended into hopelessness, as is so often the case. She grew up with a false sense of guilt, blaming herself for the abuse. Her teenage years were fraught. She grew up in an underprivileged area of Galway, did poorly at school and started to drink at an early age.

She grew steadily more depressed. Drink and drugs were taking over her life. She was self-harming; her scars were pitiful. The family doctor put her on anti-depressants. They helped to a certain extent but of course could not remove the root cause: the abuse she'd suffered in childhood.

Una Black, a damaged individual, left home at nineteen. She went from relationship to relationship, until eventually she met a man more caring than most. He was in his forties with a daughter of four. They set up home together in Walter Macken Flats, Mervue, Galway, in 2003.

She also made the acquaintance of a neighbour, John Malone, a native of County Offaly. The two had become friends almost from the time she, her partner and his daughter had moved into the apartment block. They often socialized together, meeting in local pubs or spending an evening at each other's home. Malone, thirty-nine, was separated from his wife and two children, lived alone and was drawing disability benefit.

Una's life continued on a relatively even keel for three more years. Her relationship with her partner had worked out well. As had her relationship with her "adopted" daughter, his little girl. Una loved children.

She also loved animals. Time and again she'd begged her partner to allow her to keep a dog but he'd consistently refused. His daughter didn't like dogs. But eventually he gave in and Una bought herself a lovely cocker spaniel pup. It cost her 200.

It was a mistake. Child and dog did not mix. The girl simply had an aversion to the puppy. He would have to go. Una was heartbroken.

But soon a solution presented itself. John Malone, on learning of Una's predicament, offered to keep the puppy in his flat. Una could buy his food, clean up after him and take him for his daily walk.

"He'll be a bit of company for me," John told her.

All went well – until Una took to her bed with a bad bout of flu. She neglected to send word to John. A week later she'd recovered sufficiently to leave her bed. She was alone on the night of 3 December when John knocked on her door. She invited him in for "a few drinks", as she frequently did.

The "few drinks" soon became a great many. The two continued to drink into the early hours. By five in the morning, both were very drunk. It was then that John began his recriminations.

"I sold that dog of yours, you know," he said.

"My puppy?"

"Well, you lost interest in him. You weren't round to see him any more. I couldn't bring him out for his walk, so I let him go."

"I was sick in my bed!" Una protested.

"Well, how was I to know that? I got a hundred and thirty-five euros for him. That's yours, of course."

"I don't want the bloody money! I want my puppy back."

"Well sorry, Una, but he's gone now."

John rose unsteadily and told her he was going back to his own flat. She could call round anytime and collect the money.

Una was incensed. She ran after him and collared him on the stairwell.

"I want my puppy!" she repeated. "Where is he?"

"Gone to a good home. A better one than you gave him."

He shoved her away. They struggled. The more they struggled the angrier Una grew. She was determined to retrieve her cocker spaniel.

What happened next she remembers but vaguely. She was drunk, was still on antidepressants, and possibly had smoked some cannabis as well. It was five-thirty.

She recalls going back to her flat in a blind fury and fetching a sharp knife from the kitchen. She was going to teach John Malone "a thing or two". She was going to "give him a fright and keep him away from me".

It did not work out as she'd planned in her drunken rage. She caught up with John as he reached the bottom of the stairs. They struggled again. Una produced the knife and lunged at him. The blade struck him in the chest. He tried to get away. Una stabbed him in the back – not once but several times. He collapsed face down on the concrete path, blood pumping from a severed artery.

The shock of seeing her neighbour and good friend mortally wounded brought Una to her senses – if only partially. At any rate she recovered sufficiently to appreciate the gravity of her situation.

She'd killed a man.

John's corpse would be found sooner or later, she reckoned. He'd been seen going into her flat earlier that night. She could become a suspect. She therefore decided to report the incident herself, if only to deflect attention from herself. Still clutching the knife, she went back to her flat and phoned the Gardaí.

"I'm after seeing men having a fight down below," she told the switchboard operator. "There's one of them lying on the ground."

The Guards who responded to the call found John Malone as Una had left him. He was still alive, if only barely. They called an ambulance. By the time it reached the hospital John was dead.

Una failed to appear at her trial in Galway on 11 April 2008. Mr Justice Paul Carney, presiding over the Central Criminal Court, heard that she'd absconded. He gave her until eleven o'clock to appear before him.

"My lord, if you don't mind . . ." a voice came from the front benches. It was Mrs Geraldine Black, Una's mother.

"Yes?" the judge asked, annoyed by the interruption.

"I'm her mother, my lord. I want to apologize for Una. It was a terrible thing she did."

"Thank you, Mrs Black."

He turned to the jury. The court, he explained to them, had put into place elaborate precautions to ensure that members of the jury were unaware of certain matters pertaining to the trial and that evidence must be presented in a proper way. This was to ensure that the trial wouldn't be prejudiced in any way. It's standard practice; it would not be the first time a jury would be dismissed on similar grounds and a fresh trial mounted. Mrs Geraldine Black, he declared, had been busily feeding information to the jury members. It would not do.

Poor Mrs Black. A month before, her younger daughter Nicola, then twenty-three, had been arrested for drunk driving and dangerous driving. She was due to appear in court in October 2008 but failed to show. The reason? She'd been arrested in Surinam, a tiny country on the northern coast of South America, for possession of cocaine. It was alleged that Nicola had strapped the drugs to her thighs before boarding a plane bound for Europe. Mrs Black would have her work cut out for her in her efforts to get diplomatic aid in the matter.

But in Una's case she'd carried her motherly concern too far. The judge was greatly displeased with Mrs Black's meddling.

"When I came into this court yesterday morning," he said, "I found that everybody had made assumptions about what I am going to do. I do not like that. Extremely strong representations have been made to the court to have the trial here in Galway and the court agreed to that. But in light of the above, the trial will now have to take place in Dublin."

The eleven o'clock deadline came and went and Una failed to show. The prosecution explained. Late on Monday evening Una had taken a ferry from Rosslare to Wales.

"Is this true?" the judge asked.

"We believe so," senior counsel said. "Whilst it is true that a return ticket had been purchased in Miss Black's name, Miss Black never actually boarded the ferry."

The judge was confused. A Garda assisted.

"We believe that Miss Black is still out of the jurisdiction and presently in Wales."

Justice Carney issued a warrant for Una's arrest. Sure enough, she was in Wales, having missed the Wednesday sailing. Police arrested her when her ferry docked in the early hours of Friday morning. In a new trial held the following month, she pleaded guilty to the charges of manslaughter.

It seemed that Una was not going to evade justice after all. However, when Mr Justice Carney was preparing to hand down her sentence in July, a letter was passed to him. It was from Una. She apologized for killing John Malone and realized she'd have to live with the guilt for the rest of her life.

She had further news for the court. She was seven months' pregnant.

Unkind words did the rounds. Una had, it was alleged, allowed herself to become pregnant in order to gain the sympathy of the court. Not so, replied her mother indignantly. It was a lie.

In the event it did not matter one way or another. The judge passed sentence and it was a harsh one: Una would spend nine years in prison, baby or no baby.

Heavily pregnant, Una began her prison term in Mountjoy at the end of July 2008 and gave birth to a baby girl a month later in the Rotunda Hospital, Dublin. She went into labour a little before midnight on the first of September and was rushed to the hospital accompanied by an armed escort. Hers was the fifteenth birth among the female prisoners at Mountjoy; others included a baby born to Charlotte Mulhall. In fact, the women's complex, the Dóchas Centre, is excellently equipped for childbirth should an emergency arise, having as it does its own nurses and a qualified midwife. While not the ideal place to raise an infant, the Centre, with its own crèche, is nevertheless child-friendly. Moreover, a mother is provided with her own "apartment" complete with en-suite bathroom.

That's not to say that a child born in jail can be held onto indefinitely. The authorities consider such children to be at risk and the policy is to remove them from the mother after about a year.

Una's mother Geraldine pledged to take over the care of the infant when the time comes. Otherwise the little girl would be handed over to social services. Mrs Black has visited her daughter and commends the accommodation.

"She's in a house which is spacious and very good for Una," she said. "I don't see any harm in Una looking after the child in prison. It's very clean and very tidy and the staff are very good."

At the same time Mrs Black does not believe Una should be in jail at all.

"She didn't kill anybody," she insisted, despite Una having confessed to the crime. "I don't accept it. I know what they say is one thing. It's going to appeal anyway."

Not according to Justice Carney it isn't. He refused leave to appeal. Una must serve out her full sentence.

10

JACQUI AND KELLY NOBLE
Take to Thee a Sharp Weapon

The year was 2000; the month was May and the place was Sandyhill Road, Ballymun. Lying in the shadow of the seven high towers, each named for a hero of the 1916 Easter Rising, Sandyhill was among the four-storey buildings constructed in the sixties to house some of the less well off in north Dublin. The flats are there no longer: they were demolished several years ago to make way for urban regeneration.

In one of the dilapidated apartments a woman named Jacqui Noble picked up a mobile phone. It did not belong to her and she was unused to handling it. She was also extremely nervous. She rang a number stored in the memory. A man's voice answered at once.

"He's asleep," she said. "I think."

"Right. You get out of there. I'm on my way."

Jacqui left without locking the flat. Some minutes later a man wearing a long overcoat nudged the door

173

open. He was the owner of the mobile phone. His name was Paul Hopkins and he lived close by in another block of flats. He worked as a doorman for a Drumcondra pub but tonight he was moonlighting, Jacqui having paid him £200. It was a down-payment on a larger sum, to be settled when Paul's work was done. That work entailed the killing of a man: her long-time partner Derek Benson.

She'd left him some weeks before, having finally plucked up the courage to escape from his influence over her. Her flight exposed her to danger of the worst kind: her spurned partner, she knew, would sooner or later exact bloody revenge. She'd taken their fourteen-year-old daughter with her. Her new home, a three-bedroomed house in nearby Knowth Court, had belonged to her parents. Now both were dead. Jacqui was waiting for her father's will to go into probate, when she'd inherit the house and a tidy sum of money.

But Benson was demanding what he regarded as his share of the inheritance. He told Jacqui there would be enough left over for him to buy an apartment, as well as the motorbike he had his eye on for some time. She was equally determined that he wouldn't see a penny of it.

Even if she had to kill him . . .

Her instincts told her that once Benson had the money he'd come looking for her and his daughter. She was mortally afraid of the consequences of that meeting. When she'd run into Paul Hopkins a day or two before, she saw him as a saviour. He could do the "wet work", and she'd supply the fee.

It was a little before three in the morning, yet the lateness of the hour did not entirely account for Benson being asleep. Earlier that night Jacqui had surreptitiously dosed him with a cocktail of heroin and Valium, sufficient to lay the big man low.

It had been relatively easy to do. Benson had visited his dentist that day and was in considerable pain when the anaesthetic wore off. Jacqui had "kindly" offered to alleviate that pain.

Paul had no qualms about ending Benson's life. He was well aware of the brutality of the man, how he'd made Jacqui's life a living hell. This was no recent occurrence either; she'd endured fourteen years of it. In Paul's eyes the man was a monster. No depravity was too low for him, it seemed. He'd heard of Jacqui's appalling injuries sustained throughout her time with Benson. He would beat her with his fists, kick her mercilessly, fracturing her ribs on more than one occasion. As if that wasn't enough he would reach for the nearest blunt instrument and batter her senseless. A doctor at the health centre in Ballymun first treated Jacqui's injuries in 1994 and she returned to him again and again, each time with fresh wounds and fractures. He saw bruises all over her body: injuries to her breasts caused by Benson's fists; injuries to her back caused by Benson's boots. No part of her anatomy was spared. He urged her many times to go to the police.

There was sexual depravity too. Benson's favourite perversion was tying her to a chair or the bed and raping her violently. To add to the horror, their young daughter was often a witness to her father's atrocities. Benson was not averse to child abuse either – as we shall see.

Jacqui secured a barring order against him in 1997. He breached it, as brutal partners often do, and vented his maniacal rage on the female police officer who arrested him. Garda Sinead Magee was on patrol that evening when she came upon Benson standing below Jacqui's flat. He was shouting abuse and demanding to be let in.

"I'll have to ask you to leave, sir," she said. "You're creating a disturbance."

"I'll create more than a disturbance if that cow doesn't open the door!"

Garda Magee noted that Benson smelled strongly of drink. Moreover his eyes were wild, pupils dilated. She recognized the signs of heavy drug abuse when she saw them. She went up to the flat to investigate. But no sooner had Jacqui opened the door than Benson shoved past her.

"There's a barring order out on him," Jacqui said. "He's not allowed in here and he knows it."

The Guard arrested him and brought him before the District Court. He was granted bail on condition that he adhered to the barring order and not molest his partner again. He appeared to assent.

But Benson's acquiescence was short-lived. Garda Magee escorted him to the custody office, made out the bail bond and handed him a pen.

"Sign, please. This is your guarantee that you'll behave yourself in future."

He laughed in her face.

"Guarantee?" he spat. "I guarantee you I'll be back in Jacqui Noble's flat tonight and she won't be making a complaint this time!"

She returned him to the courtroom and informed the judge. Bail was at once revoked. Benson would spend the night in the cells.

But he was not a man to have two women insult him on the same evening. As Garda Magee ushered him up to the cells he swung around and struck her, attempting to knock her down the stairs. She summoned help and Benson was arrested. He was charged with assaulting a police officer and given a six-month prison sentence. But somehow he gained access to heroin and tried to overdose in an effort to escape punishment. The attempt failed.

Paul Hopkins, assassin in the making, did not believe for a moment that Jacqui Noble's accusations against her partner were unfounded. He knew Benson for the brute he was. He and his girlfriend had suffered verbal abuse from the man on a number of occasions. Benson had assaulted him violently. Worst of all was the threat he'd levelled at Paul's girlfriend and their baby daughter. His words were chilling.

"When I've finished with them I'll burn them."

Paul inferred from this that Benson intended to rape mother and daughter before killing them.

He vowed it would never come to that. When he was through, Benson would be incapable of any more acts of violence. He'd be incapable of anything.

Paul opened his coat and slid out the sword his brother had sold him for £50. He considered it to be a rare bargain. The Wushu blade was over thirty inches long and it curved impressively from a circular, brass-plated hand guard. The wooden pommel felt good to the touch. Paul had no idea what the Chinese ideograms etched on the blade meant but imagined them to be an invocation to some dark and bloodthirsty deity.

The blade glinted brightly in the fluorescent light from the ceiling, and it was this glinting that brought the semicomatose Benson to his senses. He caught sight of the sword – and saw murder in Paul Hopkins's eyes.

The blade flashed down. Benson screamed.

The sword had sliced into his middle.

"For fuck's sake!" he screeched, and screeched again.

His screams rose ever higher as the blade cut through his body: limbs, torso, any part of his anatomy that Paul could reach. Terrified neighbours in adjoining flats thought that a pig was being slaughtered.

The kitchen did indeed resemble an abattoir, and the animal being slaughtered was what men in the Orient call a "long pig". Paul steadied his sword-arm for the final cut, the coup de grâce that would silence his victim's howls of agony.

He hacked at the neck, practically severing it from the body. Blood fountained up from the ruined arteries. Benson died.

The pathologist who examined the mutilated corpse would count no fewer than twenty-five stab wounds and sixty deep lacerations to the head, torso and limbs, *some of which went right through the body*. The man was almost cut in half in places. Dr Cassidy noted in particular a "gaping wound" that cut through to the cervical spine, the vertebrae connecting the neck to the head.

The mission was accomplished and it was time for Paul to leave. He wasn't quite done, however: his DNA would surely be present in the flat, perhaps even on the corpse. He had to destroy that evidence. He set fire to the flat. It wasn't part of the plan however.

As the place began to fill with smoke, he slipped out and down to street level. A neighbour raised the alarm and within minutes the Fire Brigade was at the scene. The blaze was put out quickly; Benson's corpse had hardly been singed.

Nor did it take the police long to track down his killer. Even though Benson, through his unsavoury reputation in Ballymun, had many enemies, Jacqui had most to gain from his death. She was interviewed and broke under questioning, thereby implicating Paul Hopkins. The Gardaí discovered the murder weapon, the Wushu sword, stashed in a closet in a friend's home. Jacqui and Paul were arrested and accused of murder.

The trial was to last thirty days. Jacqui's defence team had amassed expert opinion on her state of mind at the time of the killing, but Mr Justice Henry Abbott refused to admit any psychiatric or psychological evidence. To Jacqui's chagrin, he also ruled out provocation as a defence. Despite the court having heard of her fourteen years of extreme mental, physical and sexual cruelty at the hands of Derek Benson, and despite the testimony of witnesses who could confirm his brutal nature – including that of Garda Sinead Magee – the judge decided that Jacqui had not been provoked into killing him.

Some might have asked whether Jacqui had an alternative. Claire Keely, who lived next door to her, gave evidence that seemed to imply that Jacqui had been virtually a prisoner of Benson. He was a tyrant and probably a psychopath as well. She told the court that on one occasion he beat Jacqui with a plank of wood for failing to get up and prepare his breakfast.

Jacqui had once used the Keely home as a temporary refuge. She fled there to escape one of Benson's murderous fits. He'd rushed in after her.

"He was killing her," Claire stated. "He was beating her on the ground in front of us."

There could be little doubt that Jacqui lived in terror of the man. Claire too had cause to fear him: he'd threatened to burn her out if she persisted with what he regarded as meddling in his private affairs. The neighbourhood shared her fear.

There was no way out for Jacqui. The barring order was useless; Benson refused to stay away. Nor could she leave *him*.

"He wouldn't allow her to," Claire informed the court. "He said he'd kill her first."

Jacqui would have had ample grounds to believe he'd carry out the threat. Statistics show that three-quarters of murders of women by their partners occur in response to the woman's attempt to leave her man. Yet she decided to risk her life and get out. She had little choice: she believed he'd kill her anyway, one way or the other.

But that constant threat could not be considered as provocation, the prosecution insisted. The crime was a well-planned and premeditated act of murder, carried out by another for a fee. The promised blood-money had been between 3,000 and 5,000. Both Paul and Jacqui vehemently rejected this.

Jacqui's pleas went unheard. The jury found the pair guilty of murder and sentenced them to life imprisonment.

It was February 2004. Those present for the trial could not have imagined that Jacqui Noble would be joined in Mountjoy Prison a little over three years later by her daughter Kelly. They'd seen the fourteen-year-old in court among family members who had wept openly as Jacqui's sentence was handed down.

They'd also heard an unsettling allegation. Not only had Benson abused her mother, he'd sexually abused the child as well. She was five or six at the time. Kelly was assessed in St Clare's Unit at Temple Street children's hospital and the unmistakable signs of abuse were found. The doctors wished to alert the Gardaí but Jacqui wouldn't hear of it. There'd been no abuse of her daughter after all, she told them; the girl had retracted the allegations.

181

Benson had "got to her", as he'd got to her mother. It appears that his perversion knew no bounds.

Some people are born unlucky. Kelly Noble was such a one. She had the great misfortune to be born to a brutal man – a dealer in heroin and counterfeit drugs and he himself a drug abuser – and to a woman who was a heroin addict.

She also underwent the trauma of seeing that woman put behind bars for plotting to kill that father. Nor was it an orthodox murder; her father had been slaughtered like a pig.

We can only speculate on the effect that reports of the butchery had on Kelly's young mind. Would she have imagined the screams, the blood, her father being hacked open while still alive? Psychologists tell us that a child that loses a parent to such barbarousness will look upon weapons in one of two ways. A knife will be either an object to be feared – or to be used for one's own ends.

Kelly evidently chose the latter course. She'd grown up in a household where casual violence was an everyday affair. She'd watched her mother being brutalized and probably could only conclude that this was the normal lot of women, that she too would have to endure this in later life. She became tough. In the words of the judge who sentenced her, she had "an appalling upbringing".

With her mother in prison, Kelly was placed in foster care. But she would always be a wayward girl. She became sexually active at an early age, had many liaisons and was pregnant at seventeen with her first child: a daughter she named Jasmine.

A council house became free in the Seaview Estate in Laytown, County Meath. Kelly was moved there. Some time later she met the man with whom she'd have a second child in 2003. The relationship did not last. And so it was that when she went shopping in the town centre on a warm evening in June 2006, she was twenty years of age, a single mother of two and living on benefits. But she augmented that small income by selling drugs. She was herself an addict, just like her dead father – Derek Benson was exercising a baleful influence from beyond the grave. In more ways than one, it seems: Kelly was not averse to the use of violence when settling an argument.

Kelly had gone with her little son Leon in a buggy to buy milk and cigarettes. She entered Pat's Centra supermarket in the town square, the store where she did the weekly shop and bought odds and ends.

In retrospect it was a case of poor timing, because some minutes later Emma McLoughlin showed up. She was with her two toddlers and accompanied by her younger sister Shona. Emma was far from sober. The two had spent the afternoon at the beach, drinking with friends. All except her had been drinking beer and cider. Emma had consumed a great quantity of vodka and several bottles of WKD and was very drunk upon her arrival at Pat's supermarket. She'd gone there to buy crisps and soft drinks for the children.

Emma was Kelly's sworn enemy; she was a girl who "thought she was someone", a quality that did not endear her to Kelly, who saw herself as hen of the walk.

"She thought she was big Miss Large," Kelly said of Emma. "I was selling drugs and she thought she was bigger than me. She was always pushing it."

Emma was indeed no shrinking violet, according to Shona. Diagnosed as having attention deficit disorder and attending counselling, the girl was prey to frequent bouts of violence, ones that needed only the slightest provocation. In June of the previous year the sisters had rowed over a mobile phone. Emma had punched Shona in the face, knocking her to the ground. She demanded the phone. Shona refused. Emma kicked her in the face, knocking her unconscious.

She came to in hospital, to be told she had a broken jaw and a swelling to the brain. From that time on Shona feared that Emma could kill her; she was that unpredictable.

The animosity between Emma and Kelly went back several years. Theirs was a feud that began over a perceived slight, which would lead to angry words, then to blows. Emma, if we're to believe Kelly, had "busted" her nose in a punch-up. She'd punched her three times. Emma had "come after" Kelly on another occasion, brandishing a hammer and terrifying Kelly's little daughter Jasmine.

The child's terror was understandable: Emma had once attacked a neighbouring twelve-year-old as well as a boy of seven. She'd even assaulted her boyfriend's father with a crowbar. She and her boyfriend had, according to a neighbour in Laytown, "an unenviable reputation".

But Kelly was far from blameless. Emma accused her of having kicked her in the abdomen when she was pregnant. It was a terrible charge.

Now she spotted her again, standing by the in-store ATM – the young woman who'd almost caused her to miscarry. She rounded on her.

"Why did you kick me in the stomach when I was pregnant?" she asked Kelly.

"Fuck off!"

"Why did you kick me in the stomach when I was pregnant?" Emma demanded again.

She struck Kelly on the nose, causing it to bleed. Kelly was incensed.

"Come outside and do that again!" she dared her.

"Why did you kick me in the stomach when I was pregnant?"

The manager intervened, coming between them.

"Ladies, ladies!" he pleaded. He turned to Emma, whom he knew too well. "You're talking about something that happened *three years ago*. Why won't you let it rest? Leave Kelly alone now."

They nodded grudgingly, Kelly holding a tissue to her bloodied nose.

"Maybe it's better if you leave," the manager told Emma. She took his advice.

He seemed to have pacified the young women. Yet in reality his well-meant words had done nothing of the sort.

The unprovoked attack on Kelly Noble was to have ferocious repercussions.

Kelly, badly shaken but resolute, refused to allow Emma McLoughlin to have her way unchallenged. She was uneasy too: she'd noticed that some members of Emma's gang had gathered outside. She'd be no match for them.

She phoned Niamh Cullen, the girl who was minding her daughter, and asked her to come to her assistance. She was to bring "a blade".

"I need something," she told her friend. "Emma McLoughlin is going to kick the head off me."

Evidently she intended to use the knife – whether to frighten Emma or to do her injury we do not know for certain. However, there were witnesses to her dark intentions.

"I'm going to slice the bitch up," she told a shop worker.

Her friend duly arrived outside the shop. By this time a considerable crowd had gathered; they comprised mainly young women and children. Niamh had brought Kelly's daughter Jasmine in her buggy, not wishing to leave the child unattended. But on the back of the buggy was a schoolbag. Inside it was a kitchen knife, the "blade" the child's mother had requested. Niamh rendezvoused with Kelly inside the store. She collected the knife and concealed it up her sleeve.

Emma was still out on the square close to the supermarket. Drunker and more wound up, she was shouting and threatening. The anger appeared to have left

Kelly, however. She wished to leave, to go home in peace. But Emma, still spoiling for a fight, impeded her.

Kelly produced the knife.

"Back the fuck off, Emma!" she warned. "I'm telling you, I'll cut you."

Emma kept on coming. Little Jasmine and Leon began to wail.

"Fight me then!" she snarled. "I'm not pregnant now."

Without further preamble, Kelly lunged at her rival. Emma tried to grab the weapon but latched onto Kelly's arm instead. She pushed her back.

"Do you think I'm scared of you?" she taunted. "Do you think I'm scared of the knife, do you? Come on: stick it in me. What the fuck – are you afraid of me?"

Then it happened. In full view of Emma's children and her own, and with a frenzied thrust, Kelly stabbed her rival in the chest. The girl collapsed, blood pouring from the wound.

"I seen Emma get stabbed," Shona McLoughlin was to testify. "When Kelly took the knife out it was full of blood."

Niamh Cullen rushed to Kelly's distraught children. She was trying to spare them the horror.

"I was trying to get the children to calm down," she says, "and not be looking."

Bystanders were aghast. A nurse was among them. Reacting quickly, she grabbed a towel from the supermarket and rushed to the stricken young woman. She pressed it down onto the wound. Yet the blood continued to seep out of Emma's ruined breast.

Calm as you please, Kelly gathered her children and headed for home, accompanied by Niamh Cullen. The friend was shaken; she hadn't expected Kelly actually to use the knife but only to threaten her rival with it.

Shona McLoughlin got on the phone to her eldest sister Edel to tell her about the tragedy. Edel called Kelly at once and demanded an explanation. The reply was brief and callous.

"She deserved it!"

Somebody had already called the emergency services. But help would be slow to arrive. Laytown is a short drive from Drogheda yet, due to circumstances beyond their control, it took some forty-five minutes for the ambulance crew to get there. By that time Emma had died in Shona's arms. In Our Lady of Lourdes Hospital, death by haemorrhaging was recorded.

There was no doubting the identity of the killer. The people of Laytown could identify her to the Gardaí when at last they arrived on the scene. They went to Kelly's home in Seaview and arrested her on a charge of murder. They were careful not to handcuff her in front of her children. The kids had been traumatized enough for one day.

Kelly sat expressionless towards the close of her trial in March 2007 as the judge pronounced sentence. She'd done her best to evade justice, had appealed to the sympathy of the court. She'd pleaded that her dreadful upbringing was a factor that had contributed to her culpability. She never had a chance.

"I got the raw end of the deal growing up," she'd said. "They knew my da had me selling drugs and was beating me, but all the Guards were afraid of him. He was a madman. He battered a Ban Garda who tried to help us, and when they arrested him for that he overdosed with heroin just to try and get out of the cell."

It was a plea from the heart and it moved others in the courtroom. But the judge was not to be swayed. Two little children had been left motherless as a result of Kelly's savage attack. Her dreadful formative years would not mitigate that fact.

"Your crime is one of manslaughter," he told her. "You murdered a young mother. That is a crime that falls within the upper range of manslaughter, for which the tariff is twelve years' imprisonment."

He then went on to speak of provocation. "You submitted two pleas: one of provocation and one of self-defence. I am obliged to sentence on the basis that the jury have accepted the defence more favourable to you, namely that of self-defence."

Finally, after a lengthy summing up, he informed Kelly he was handing down a ten-year sentence. He was taking into account the fact that she showed remorse. Furthermore, she herself was the mother of two young children, and she'd made attempts to deal with her drug addiction.

"However, the last two will be suspended and the sentence backdated to June 2006. Therefore, you will serve a total of eight years. Take her down."

Surely there were few in that courtroom who did not associate mother and daughter being sent to jail for the taking of life – and prayed that the violence would not continue into a third generation.

So Kelly joined her mother in the Dóchas Centre, Mountjoy: two women joined by blood. She also joined two other women whose bloody crime had held a nation in thrall: Linda and Charlotte Mulhall, the killers of the Kenyan who'd abused their mother and who would surely have started on the elder sister had they not ended his life with great violence.

But Kelly would serve a far lesser sentence than would her mother – even though her mother had not wielded the blade that snuffed out the life of another human being, and her daughter had. In February 2008 an appeal court slashed two years off her prison time with a further two suspended, on the grounds that her ten-year sentence was one reserved for criminal acts on the "high end" of the scale. It was decided that Kelly's crime lay somewhere in the middle of that scale. Furthermore she'd admitted to man-slaughter even before the trial began, and that, her defence team contended, had not been taken into consideration. Psychologists have also concluded that there's a low risk of her re-offending upon release.

Not that she's any angel. There was a grisly twist to the tale when Kelly joined her mother in Mountjoy's

Dóchas Centre: the residents were curious about the young woman who was to join her mother behind bars. In fact the two acquired something resembling celebrity status among the inmates. This apparently did not sit well with the Mulhall sisters. After all, were they not Ireland's most notorious female prisoners?

The rivalry between the Nobles and the Mulhalls grew more intense by the day. Eventually it would come to blows. The prison authorities intervened and Kelly was transferred to the stricter confines of Limerick Prison.

It is possible that she'll be released in 2012 – it is far from easy to predict how the wheels of justice will turn. Her mother Jacqui, however, will still be behind bars on that date, serving out the remainder of her fourteen years.

11

SHARON GRACE
The Drownings in Wexford

It was a fine Sunday morning in April 2005 when a party of anglers set out to do a spot of fishing on Kaats Strand, a stretch of shoreline on the north of Wexford Harbour. Toddy Roche was among them.

"What's that?" asked one of his friends, indicating something in the shallows. It resembled a hand.

Toddy squatted down to investigate. What he saw filled him at first with curiosity, then with increasing horror. The hand belonged to a woman whose corpse lay face up under the water. Next to her was the body of a little girl, also face up. To add to the grisly find, the body of a toddler lay between the child and the woman. Toddy immediately called the police. They responded to the summons at once. The Gardaí are on call around the clock, seven days a week.

Other essential services are not.

The previous evening, Sharon Grace left her home in the little village of Barntown and took a taxi to Ely Hospital. It's a private medical centre about a half-mile from Kaats Strand. Sharon knew that it's also where Wexford's social workers are based. Her two younger daughters, four-year-old Mikahla and Abby, three, accompanied her.

Sharon was depressed. She was seeking help, someone who, in her father's words, "could have brought her in, sat her down, given her a cup of tea and chatted with her".

It didn't happen. It didn't happen because there was no one who could see her. Sharon learned at the hospital desk that social workers were on duty only from nine to five, Monday to Friday. It was seven-thirty in the evening, and it was Saturday.

"If you want to come back on Monday morning," the receptionist said. "Or I can contact Wexford hospital and see if someone's available."

"No, don't bother," said the unhappy woman.

Taking her two girls by the hand, Sharon left the hospital.

We can only speculate what was going through the twenty-nine-year-old's head as she left the building. The receptionist, Marian Redmond, was concerned for her. She saw how disturbed Sharon was. Marian was accustomed to seeing patients with psychiatric problems and knew the signs. She wished she could have been of more help, but her hands were tied. There was no one at the Ely.

She watched the visitor as she turned out at the hospital gate. It was ten past eight and already dark. Marian looked out of the window and saw Sharon walking in the direction of Castle Bridge, which connects the town to its northern shore. Sharon had little Abby in her arms, with Mikahla following on her heels. The woman seemed unhurried and calm.

The receptionist was not to know that within the hour all three would be dead. Sharon Grace had made her way purposefully to the water's edge at Kaats Strand. We can only wonder about what she said to the girls when she stopped on the grass overlooking the shallows. The water is only three feet deep at this point, but enough to drown a child in. She would still have been clutching three-year-old Abby. Did she take Mikahla by the hand and jump? Did she tell them it was a game?

The little girls would have known within moments that it was certainly no game, as their desperate mother held their heads under the cold, dark water and they struggled for survival. We cannot know what anguish Sharon felt as she snuffed out the lives of the children so close to her heart. We can only hope that they did not suffer too much – the three of them, because Sharon submerged herself next to her girls when their struggles had ended.

The tragedy might well have been avoided. Only the day before, two social workers had visited her at her home in Barntown. They surely must have seen how depressed she was: it had been going on a long time. It's difficult to avoid the conclusion that suicide was not too far from Sharon's thoughts at that time.

Yet to be fair, suicide cannot be predicted in the majority of cases – if it can be predicted at all. To state the obvious: we cannot possibly know what's going on in the mind of another. The social workers could not have predicted that Sharon was planning to kill herself. They most certainly could not have imagined that she'd take her two youngest children with her, the involuntary participants in a multiple drowning.

The problem is compounded by the fact that depression by itself does not induce a person to take her own life. But a sense of *hopelessness* does. Hope is what keeps us going, the conviction that the world will look better in the morning.

In all likelihood Sharon saw the Ely clinic as her last hope. When even that hope evaporated she was close to despair. She didn't show it because her mind was already made up, hence her look of determination as she left the hospital with her children. She knew she'd reached the end of the line and was reconciled to the fact. Who knows but she may even have been contented. Suicide by its very nature is the final act, the final choice. Sometimes it can be the final opportunity a woman can have to take control of her life, to decide her own destiny without interference from others. The tragedy, of course, lies in the finality of that control. In Sharon's case the tragedy was tripled as she took two lives besides her own.

Widower Barry Grace remains unhappy with social services in his area, insisting that they're still inadequate, as they were on that terrible night when he lost a wife and two children.

"The problem is not the people who work in the social services," he believes, "but the lack of funding and resources in the area. We just don't have the resources here to deal with it."

He alludes to Adrian Dunne of Enniscorthy who, two years after Sharon's death, is alleged to have killed his wife and two young daughters before hanging himself. He'd gone to an undertaker a week before in order to make funeral arrangements. Barry says this should have sounded the warning bells.

"The Gardaí were involved," he says. "They should have got a social worker and visited the family home. They should have made sure there was a professional there to assess the situation. The HSE said they'd sent somebody to the home but it wasn't a social worker, somebody trained to be able to spot if there are any problems."

The HSE had alerted the gardaí but a detective had sent a priest to investigate. He in turn had requested the parish priest to visit.

"Priests were not the right people to be sent," Barry argues. "Gardaí and social workers should have gone directly to the house themselves. Maybe then the situation would not have escalated like it did."

Maybe. But a year after the Wexford drownings Sharon Grace's sister Lillian broke her silence. She contended that social services were being unjustly blamed. The inquest into the tragedy, she said, had failed to provide details of a meeting Sharon had had with a female social worker at Ely Hospital on Monday, 16 April, five days before the drownings.

Lillian had driven her sister to the clinic. She states that Sharon was "absolutely terrified" at the prospect that she might lose her children, that Barry would gain custody of them. Lillian assured her that social services could provide a solution.

"Sharon had never been in touch with them before," she says. "She was there about forty minutes, and then all of a sudden she came out again and she said to me: 'Thank God for that, Lilly. She was really nice. There was no bother at all.'"

Apparently the social worker gave Sharon to understand there was no question of her losing her children. She advised her on how to go about getting a legal separation, a move that would give her enhanced custody rights.

"The girl made Sharon feel really at ease and comfortable," Lillian recalls, "saying she was a good mother. She told her, 'At the end of the day we're here for the kids.'"

So clearly there was hope and Sharon was aware of that. Evidently something occurred between the Monday and Saturday that caused her to abandon that hope. We shall probably never know what that something was.

12

MARY KEEGAN
The House of Fear

"There's something in this house . . . She won't let anyone help you. Even if someone came, what can they do? They'll only become trapped as well."
"She started acting really strange . . . She's a danger to herself, and us . . . I told you: she won't let us leave."
"She went insane and committed suicide."

Fear House, *2008*

One of the more disturbing horror films of 2008 was *Fear House*. Set in an isolated house in the Californian desert, it features a reclusive novelist named Samantha Ballard who's been missing for nine months. Her friends and relatives – including her ex-husband – eventually discover her whereabouts. Samantha is not herself; something terrible has occurred; something has caused her to lose her mind.

"You will not leave this house alive," she tells them. And lo, the deaths begin. First to die, and to die most horribly, are her ex-husband and his girlfriend. Somehow the house knows exactly what it is each of the visitors fears most – and goes out of its way to prey upon that fear. No one can escape: the gates are chained up.

Fear House is not a particularly good movie; Hollywood has made much better movies in the genre. Yet it creeps us out; we share the terror of the house's victims. On that level the film works well.

Best of all, we know that when the final credits roll we're safe to go about our business or pleasure. We believe there are no such "fear houses" in real life.

We would be wrong, as two little boys discovered in February 2006.

Firhouse is pronounced Fear House by many who live there. The name may derive from *fir*, Irish for "of the man". Equally Firhouse may have been named after a manor house that once stood there and whose driveway was lined with fir trees.

Killakee Walk is a quiet cul-de-sac tucked into the northern end of Firhouse. It's a pleasant little street on the south-western periphery of the city with the foothills of the Dublin Mountains forming a rural backdrop.

Nothing much happens in Killakee Walk. Hardworking couples commute to the city via the M50 that runs close by; children attend local schools, join local sports clubs; groceries are bought at the local SuperValu and other shops; Mass is said in Our Lady of Mount Carmel; Sunday service is conducted in the Glorious Family church. Killakee Walk is a family-orientated kind of place. So far, so ordinary.

Yet on a May evening in 1998 the quietude of this peaceful corner of Firhouse was shattered and its innocence lost for ever. Two youths quarrelled over a girl. Tara Ryan was visiting a friend, Stephen Morris, at his home. The doorbell rang. It was Tara's boyfriend Vincent Flynn, aged nineteen. He'd learned of her visit and was consumed by jealousy – she'd already told him she "fancied" the handsome and personable Stephen. Determined to "sort out" his love rival, Vincent had brought along a hunting knife with an eight-inch blade.

Outside the house in Killakee Walk the two youths had a flaming row. Vincent stabbed Stephen through the heart. The seventeen-year-old died within minutes.

It transpired that his young killer was delusional. Having collected the knife, he'd run wildly through Firhouse, claiming – of all things – to be Jesus Christ. He was sentenced to life imprisonment for the murder.

That year in Ireland there would be on average two deaths each month by stabbing. But the epidemic would peter out over time. The years passed by peacefully in Killakee Walk. The senseless stabbing faded from the residents' memories; the wounds were healing.

Not for Stephen's distraught mother. There was no time limit on her grief; she could not come to terms with her boy's untimely and brutal death. In 2004, six years after the killing, she drowned herself by walking into the sea.

But two years later the quiet cul-de-sac would be rocked by an even greater calamity, one accompanied by extreme violence and excruciating death. A family would implode.

Brian Keegan loved his wife and children. He'd worked hard to give them a good life in the suburbs. Born in 1963, he'd grown up in Rathfarnham at a time when that district was on the rim of the urban sprawl southwards. He'd met Mary Flynn, the girl he was to marry in 1992, at a social. They were near-neighbours. When the spacious, four-bedroomed house in Killakee Walk came on the market in 1995 he judged it to be perfect for rearing a family. By 2006 they'd settled in beautifully and seamlessly. They had two boys. Ten-year-old Glenn was "a rising star" with St Enda's under-11s GAA hurling team and played soccer for the local club, Firhouse Carmel. His coaches predicted that he'd one day be part of an All-Ireland line-up. His young brother Andrew, aged six, was following in Glenn's footsteps. Their mother actively encouraged her boys in sport, always being on hand to drive them to events and cheer them on from the sidelines.

Mary was a model wife and mother. After the birth of her elder son she'd turned her back on a successful full-time career in finance in order to devote more time to homemaking. In 2006 she was working part time for Woodchester, an investments house in the city centre close

201

to St Patrick's Cathedral. Her colleagues knew her as a bubbly, personable woman. If she had problems she was careful not to allow them to interfere with her work.

Her husband Brian was a respected senior employee with Broderick Grass Machinery, a mechanized garden-tool centre based then in Dún Laoghaire, but since relocated to Rathcoole, County Dublin.

Between them Brian and Mary earned enough to ensure a high standard of living for the family. In fact they were the envy of many who knew them. They seemed to have it all: a fine house, a good income, two lovely boys, and their health.

That last was deceptive, however. While Mary's physical well-being was excellent, it was otherwise with her mental state. Few outside the immediate family circle knew this. Few knew that she had a history of depression, and that her condition had worsened considerably at the end of 2005. She became convinced they'd overspent at Christmas. In the New Year her depression had deepened alarmingly. Nor did it help that the month of January was the dullest since 1999, with precious few sunny days to lift Mary's spirits. Yet somehow she managed to "put on a happy face" and keep her black feelings of hopelessness and despair to herself.

In hindsight it becomes clear that Mary Keegan was a time bomb waiting to explode.

The boys' father should have been there. He'd been on a week-long business trip to the United States. With

September's Ryder Cup golf tournament already in the planning, Broderick's had sent him to source state-of-the-art grass-cutting machines for the greens and fairways of the K Club in Kildare. Brian had planned on returning on Sunday, 12 February, in good time to organize a St Valentine's Day celebration with his beloved Mary. And multi-talented Glenn would be doing a star turn on Monday night in his school's production of *Snow White and the Seven Dwarfs* at the Civic Theatre in Tallaght. Brian had much to look forward to upon his return.

But the elements were to conspire against him. Freak winter conditions in the USA would delay his plane by twenty-four hours.

Never mind. He'd be back in time. For the panto *and* for Valentine's Day.

In the meantime, something seemed to be amiss in the Keegan home. No one had seen Mary and the boys since Friday. She'd looked in on a neighbour as she always did. They'd chatted while her boys were visiting their friends in the street. If she was feeling under the weather then she didn't show it.

"Mary was relaxed and didn't have a care in the world," the neighbour said. "She was talking about what was on the telly, and we had a cup of tea and talked about a few things. Then she headed off."

She was collecting little Andrew at his best friend's home, a few houses away. George Tobin, the lad's father, recalls her suggesting that the two youngsters take their bicycles out next day, weather permitting.

"Mary was lovely," he says. "Very attractive and focused on her children. She really looked out for the lads."

Having collected Andrew on the way home, Mary shut the door behind them. As darkness fell, she drew the blinds on the windows.

But the blinds remained drawn *all* that weekend. As the other residents came and went in Killakee Walk, as night turned to day and then to night again, there was no sign of life from the Keegan home. Neighbours reported seeing Brian's van and Mary's car in the driveway. They thought nothing of the blinds being down. People did that all the time for privacy.

Monday was a different story, though. The boys should have turned up for school and were missed. Glenn more than Andrew: the drama group were doing a final run-through of *Snow White*. Where was their singing star?

The drama teacher had someone telephone the house. The phone rang out. Others had been phoning the house since Saturday but nobody picked up. The landline was silent; Mary's mobile remained unanswered; urgent text messages went unheeded. Brian had rung several times; on receiving no reply he'd assumed that Mary had left the boys with a neighbour and was visiting friends or relatives. She was not; her relatives grew concerned. Her father, John Flynn, contacted Mary's sister Liz and together they went to investigate. John rang the doorbell.

On his receiving no answer, Liz looked through the letterbox. What she saw filled her with dread. There were bloody footprints in the hallway.

"I knew something bad had happened," she said, "because I could smell the blood. It smelled like an operating theatre." She was familiar with the odour of blood; she was a nurse and had assisted at a great many operations.

They hurried to a neighbour: Declan Whelan, a Garda. As luck would have it he was off duty that day. He took charge at once, called the station and requested that they contact the emergency services. A squad car and an ambulance were on their way within minutes.

Meanwhile Mary's sister and the off-duty Guard had gone round to the rear of the semi-detached house, to find the back door locked as well. They peered in through the kitchen window.

And wished they hadn't.

Much later, Garda forensics experts would attempt to piece together the last moments of Mary Keegan and her sons. The picture that emerged was blood-chilling. Evidently the slaughter had taken place on the Saturday, probably in the morning. It was impossible to say which of the boys was attacked first.

"Handprints and grab marks on the counters in the kitchen show there was a terrible struggle," an expert said.

The following scenario, based on the evidence gathered in the house, is an indication of how terrible that struggle must have been.

Two little boys are sitting at the kitchen table eating the breakfast their mother has prepared for them. Six-year-old Andrew is disappointed: the sunshine his mother hoped for has not materialized after all. There'll be no bike riding today: he'll have no opportunity to practise his favourite pastime of "pulling skids".

Without warning their mother gets up and locks the back door. She has a strange look in her eye. The boys have never seen it before. She goes out and they hear her locking the front door too. She returns, shutting the kitchen door behind her.

Before they know what's happening, the mother has gone to a knife block and slid out two of the biggest, sharpest carving knives she can find. She advances on the boys, brandishing a blade in each hand. The boys are terrified, not believing what is happening.

They try to run to the door. The mother hurries to bar their way. They start to scream, and race for the back door. She follows, lunges with one of the knives and it pierces the back of a fleeing boy. He shrieks. Blood flows. She stabs him again, and again, using both knives now. He staggers to the worktop and tries to prop himself up. But his mother hacks at him several more times. He falls to the tiled floor, twenty stab wounds in his body. He dies struggling for life.

His little brother is beyond fear or coherent thought. He cannot even cry out any more as his mother advances on him. She plunges the knives into his body. He slips on his dead brother's blood and falls. She stabs him again. He goes limp.

The mother is wailing, not believing what she's just done. Her grief is total. There's nothing else for it but to end her own life. She opens the kitchen door again and walks down the hallway, leaving bloody footprints in her wake. She goes upstairs to the medicine cupboard and returns with her medication. In the kitchen, standing in the blood of her murdered boys, she swallows all the pills. With one of the knives she slits her left wrist. But death is too long in coming. She hauls the knife across her windpipe, while plunging the other into her abdomen. She's dead within seconds.

Long before Brian Keegan arrives home his entire family has been wiped out.

Mary, in her delusion, had convinced herself that the Keegans were nearly on the breadline. Her greatest fear was that before long they'd find themselves on the street, penniless. She had often voiced this fear to her husband. It had grown into an obsession. Other delusions had preceded it. Mary had suffered from mental illness for many years, although few outside her immediate family circle were aware of this. She knew how to put on a brave face to the outside world. She knew how to suffer in silence.

Given what we know about suicide it's highly likely that Mary was contemplating it for some time: perhaps weeks, perhaps months. Suicide rarely comes out of the blue. No doubt her depression was a contributing factor. As we have seen, a person about to kill themselves will not necessarily appear woebegone and desperate. More likely they will appear happy – or if not happy, contented.

They will have made up their minds, have resolved to end it all.

Not even her immediate neighbours would have been aware of the turmoil in Mary's head. They saw a normal mother and her children going on with their daily lives.

"I can see them now," a neighbour recalls. "The boys would be riding their bikes on the grass and she would be there, watching them. Mary was a great mother. She never took her eyes off the kids, and she had a nice word for everybody."

No one could have guessed on Friday afternoon that the weekend would end in such tragedy and horror. Mary and Andrew had gone to watch ten-year-old Glenn play a hurling match with his St Enda's team-mates. Those who met his mother at the fixture say they had no inkling of what she'd planned for later. She was her usual seemingly happy self: "a bubbly woman".

Brian Keegan need not blame himself for not being there to prevent what occurred. In all likelihood Mary would have gone through with it regardless, when opportunity presented itself. His American trip was simply a case of bad timing. He could not have known her true state of mind then.

Probably the best analysis of her mental condition was offered by Professor Henry Kennedy, a psychiatrist who gave evidence at the inquest. In his opinion Mary was in the grip of a deep depression in the weeks preceding the tragedy. Somehow she'd managed to conceal this from all who knew her, with the possible exception of her loving husband Brian.

Professor Kennedy had examined the medical records. From them he deduced that Mary was dangerously delusional: she genuinely believed that she and her family were impoverished. She feared that her children would suffer from this poverty for the rest of their lives.

"Although she was aware of her actions on the day of the killings," he said, "she may not have been able to understand the consequences of those actions."

"I believe she knew the nature and quality of her actions in a literal sense," he went on, "but because of the delusions and abnormal thoughts, she was unable to reason about the act or its consequences."

He was saying, in effect, that Mary was mentally ill. Indeed he stated that, had she survived the killing of her sons, she'd have been declared insane "under current laws".

Professor Kennedy was alluding to a change in Irish legislation that took place the previous year with the introduction of the Criminal Law Insanity Act. As we shall see, it was because of this new legislation that psychiatrist Lynn Gibbs, who drowned her daughter in 2006, escaped jail but was committed to a mental institution. Had Mary survived, then she'd likewise have been committed.

It is shocking and beyond comprehension when such tragedies occur in our own country, in our own time. It is impossible to imagine Brian Keegan's loss. In truth it ranks as a loving father and husband's very worst nightmare.

And it is to Brian's everlasting credit that he was, despite the pain she'd caused him, able to find it in his heart to forgive her. His words, as he set them down in a statement, are moving, and should act as example to those others who find themselves in such a situation.

"There is no anger in my heart towards her," he wrote. "Her actions were born out of a will to protect our children from a harshness she perceived in the world, however inconceivable or incomprehensible this may appear to us. I would like to state clearly that I am proud to have known Mary."

"She was," he continued, "the most loving and generous person I have ever met and she was an inspiration to me and our beautiful children, Glenn and Andrew."

We have grown almost accustomed in recent years to tragedies similar to that which befell the Keegan family. And yet they continue to appal us by the unnatural character of such killings. We're inclined to believe that a mother is the last person to wish to harm her children.

Mothers killing their sons is nothing new, however. There was a time when we used to associate such killings with the United States. "Only in America," we would say. And to an extent we were correct, but alas Ireland is catching up fast. The Keegan case would not, however, be complete without referencing an American case. The parallels are striking. It happened in Texas ten years before the Firhouse tragedy.

Darlie Routier, twenty-six, blonde and pretty, had it all. Or, better said, at one time had it all. The Dallas housewife had a handsome husband and three boys. In June 1996, one was six, another five and the third just an infant. They lived in Rowlett, a fashionable suburb of the city. Their home was big and boasted an expensive redwood spa hot tub. They also owned a costly boat and Darlie's husband Darin drove a top-of-the-range Jaguar.

But a lavish lifestyle would eventually eat into their finances. At the beginning of the year they found themselves in debt; by June it was touch-and-go whether they could keep up their mortgage payments. Such was Darlie's feeling of desperation that she attempted suicide. She went on medication for depression.

On a humid night in June, Darlie's husband, who had been sleeping upstairs with the baby, came down to the kitchen to a scene of carnage. His two older sons lay dead, their little bodies lacerated with stab wounds. Darlie lay unconscious next to them. Her throat was slashed, as was one of her wrists.

When she came to, she claimed that an intruder had attacked them. Nobody believed her. Why should her shallow wounds be so inconsistent with the deep ones inflicted on the dead boys? She was tried for murder and is still on death row pending her latest appeal.

Darlie still insists she is innocent. She knows what happened that night in Dallas. Perhaps she alone knows; perhaps there was no intruder. Yet the fact remains that she had a motive – an insanely delusional motive to be sure, yet a motive nonetheless. Perhaps in the end she will relent, repent and confess it.

We shall never uncover Mary Keegan's motive for killing her own little boys. She took that with her to a grave in the grounds of the Church of the Holy Spirit in Ballyroan – the church where she and Brian were wed fourteen years before.

The boys lie next to her. They'll be remembered for a long time, in particular by their young friends. Andrew was little more than a baby, missing his First Holy Communion by two months; he never had the chance to achieve what Glenn had. For Glenn was a legend in Firhouse – or a "ledge" to his pals. He won't be forgotten, if his memorial page on Bebo was anything to go by.

"Naw One Day Goes Bie Wirou Me Thinkin Of Yu Bud," a young girl calling herself Lady GaGa inscribed in the inimitable youth-speak of Tallaght. "iLoveYou Rip XxXxxxX."

13

LYNN GIBBS
The Psychiatrist who Drowned her Girl

Gerard Gibbs had his first inkling that all was not well when he opened his front door. He was met by silence. No sound of a television, no radio, no music from Ciara's room.

"Lynn?"

No answer. Puzzled, he looked into the downstairs rooms and kitchen. There were many rooms. Gerard and Lynn's home was the envy of their neighbours; the finest in Killure in rural Kilkenny, a house built by two working professionals who saw it only in the evening and at weekends. But it was Sunday morning and the house should have been buzzing. There was no sign of life. His puzzlement grew.

It was late November 2006 and the family were already in Christmas mode. Only the previous evening Gerard's daughter Ciara had texted him in this regard. She was disappointed, she wrote. She and her brother Gearóid wished to buy a fur coat for their mother as a Christmas gift but she'd been unable to find a suitable one.

It was, he knew, "just like Ciara". Even Lynn had conceded that Ciara was "perfect". Few could argue with this.

She was sixteen, tall, slim and chestnut-haired. She had a multitude of gifts. She excelled at music and art – and just about every other school subject. But mathematics was her special talent. Ciara's gift had been spotted early and she'd been earmarked for greatness. The following summer she was to travel to the Mathematical Olympiad to be held in Hanoi, Vietnam. She'd be up against the finest young minds on the planet.

In preparation her mother had enrolled her in a special maths course for gifted students, run at NUI in Maynooth. Only the previous day – the Saturday – Lynn had accompanied her there while Gerard and Gearóid stayed with Lynn's mother-in-law.

Now Gerard was coming home to a chill, empty house. It made no sense.

"Where do you think they are?" Gearóid asked.

Gerard shook his head. He climbed the stairs, his son following.

The door to the master bedroom was open and a light burned in the en-suite bathroom.

"Lynn?" Gerard called again.

His wife was slumped on the bed. She was semiconscious. He went to her – but something even more disturbing caught his eye. It was Ciara. She was lying in a heap in the doorway to the en-suite bathroom. She looked to be asleep.

She was not. He touched the girl's cheek and it was cold. Her clothing was damp – even wet in places. He noted that the bath was full. It was then he saw a meat cleaver on the floor. There was blood on it.

He carried Ciara out to the bedroom.

Gerard did not know what to think. His anxiety mounting, he laid his daughter on the bed next to her mother. He touched Lynn. Her clothing was likewise damp. But she had a strong pulse. He turned to his son.

"Quick, Gearóid, get help!"

The fourteen-year-old hurried back down the stairs while Gerard turned his attention to his daughter. She wasn't breathing. He tried mouth-to-mouth resuscitation, but to no avail. Ciara was dead.

Out on the road a panic-stricken Gearóid flagged down a motorist. The man was on his way to Mass.

"Come quick!" the boy cried. "There's been an accident at our house."

They drove through the electronic gates that guarded the Gibbses' home. Upstairs in the main bedroom they found Gearóid's father in deep shock. He'd failed to resuscitate his sixteen-year-old daughter. Now his attention was on Lynn. She still lay next to her dead daughter; she was drifting in and out of consciousness. The neighbour noted that the clothing of both women was wet.

"My nephew's the chemist," he said. "I'll see if he's home."

He returned with his nephew and his wife, a nurse. They immediately called an ambulance, then examined the two victims. The nurse decided it was too late for Ciara but her mother had come round. She was conscious but incoherent, in a state of nervous collapse. She had a wound to her throat, evidently made by a knife or other blade, and an ugly red weal on her left wrist. Her attacker must have escaped before he could conclude his task of double murder. The ambulance arrived. The paramedics took one look at the scene and telephoned the Gardaí in Thomastown.

There was no sign of a break-in. Whoever was responsible for the assaults must have been known to Lynn Gibbs and her daughter. Had a stranger attempted to bypass the electronic gates a silent alarm would have alerted the security company. There had been no such alert. Nor had a stranger tampered with the house alarm.

Lynn was out of harm's way, but one thing was certain: it would be a time before she could offer a lucid account of what had happened. She was taken to St Luke's General Hospital and sedated. Evidently her trauma had been great.

Meanwhile Ciara had been pronounced dead. She'd been drowned: most likely in the Gibbses' own bathtub. Her body showed the marks of a struggle but offered no clue to the identity of her assailant or assailants. The Gardaí requested that Gerard and his son vacate their home while forensic experts examined it. They found nothing out of the ordinary. It was a "clean" crime scene.

Who, detectives asked, had last seen Lynn and her daughter? A woman came forward: Dr Marese Cheasty, a friend and work colleague of Lynn's. She had, she said, visited Lynn on the Saturday evening. The detectives heard how Lynn had confided to Dr Cheasty her concerns about her daughter Ciara.

"Mrs Gibbs had become extremely depressed," the doctor said. "She was worrying out of proportion about Ciara. She said the girl wasn't eating."

During the course of the interview the detectives learned that Ciara was possibly suffering from anorexia. This apparently was her mother's conviction.

"Lynn was taking her to see a specialist about her health," Cheasty said. "But Ciara was unhappy about it. She didn't think there was anything wrong with her eating habits."

Lynn was not yet ready to be interviewed. Far from it. A medical examination revealed that she'd overdosed on prescription drugs. There was also evidence of self-harming. In all likelihood she'd used the bloodstained cleaver on herself. Such was her trauma that it was decided to move her to a Dublin psychiatric hospital: St Patrick's near Kilmainham.

The Garda investigation was put on hold. All attempts to uncover evidence of the presence of an intruder on the night of 26 November had turned up nothing. They concluded that he did not exist. There could be no mistake: when Gerard Gibbs entered his home that Sunday morning,

Ciara's killer was still in the house – and slumped semiconscious on her own bed.

The pharmacist and his sister, the nurse who'd examined Lynn and Ciara, were arguably the first of the Gibbses' neighbours to penetrate the privacy of the family. The Gibbses did not mix. So isolated were they from the rural community of Killure that several neighbours weren't even aware that the couple had children. Ciara and Gearóid were kept indoors as much as possible. When a family turns in on itself to that extent, difficulties will present themselves sooner or later.

The trouble began that summer, soon after Ciara had sat her Junior Certificate examination. She'd done exceptionally well: ten A's, placing her at the head of her class – and indeed among the brightest pupils ever to sit the exam. As a reward her parents allowed her to participate in a student-exchange programme: she went to France for a fortnight.

But the unaccustomed cuisine did not agree with Ciara. She ate little and returned home considerably thinner than when she'd left. Her mother was concerned and took her to a specialist in eating disorders. Ciara resented this and her resentment served only to exacerbate the situation. She wished to be left alone to lead her own life. But her mother knew better. She herself had fought – and overcome – demons of like hue and destructive nature.

To try to understand the reasons that drove Lynn to take the life of the girl she loved, it is necessary to examine her own life.

She was born Lynn Hutchinson. Her parents, Henry and Iris, were a prosperous couple who owned an extensive farm in Ballyknockane, Ballypatrick, County Tipperary, some miles to the northwest of Carrick-on-Suir.

By most accounts Lynn's childhood was far from normal. She was troubled by an overbearing mother who had mental problems. Lynn was a quiet, shy girl who loved sports. It's common for a reserved child to seek expression in sport; the physical activity allows all those pent-up emotions free rein.

Lynn's relationship with her mother was difficult. Iris Hutchinson had a very poor self-image. She suffered from depression for many years. It culminated in her killing herself by swallowing weedkiller in 1982. She was forty-nine; Lynn was twenty-two at the time and at university.

But long before this Iris had exerted an unhealthy influence over her daughter. In her mother's eyes Lynn was a failure: not pretty enough, not bright enough, too wayward, too lazy. Too this, too that. The outcome of such overbearingness was to an extent predictable: at the age of seventeen, Lynn developed anorexia.

Clinically speaking it's an interesting complaint. Although some may regard it as being of "our" time, it was actually diagnosed as a disease in 1870s' America. Moralists were partly to blame for its proliferation among young women. The clue to this lies in the word "carnal". It literally means "of meat" but of course we tend to associate carnality with sexuality. And so it was that an overindulgence in meat was frowned upon by respectable Victorian ladies. The thin lady soon became the ideal to strive towards; thin meant spiritual purity and a life of self-denial.

We know better now and recognize eating disorders for what they are: a cry for help. The child psychologist Oliver James suggests that a mixed-up parent can trigger an eating disorder:

In later life, having a perfectionist mother predicts a greater likelihood of bulimia if the daughter has low self-esteem. Mothers of bulimics are liable to be belittling and censorious, and since these are both significant causes of depression it is not surprising that bulimics are liable to suffer from it.

By contrast, anorexics tend to have confusing mothers who give mixed messages, similar to the mystifying "double-binds" in which parents of schizophrenics may place their children. Indeed, compared with bulimics anorexics are more liable to have delusions, which are a defining symptom of schizophrenia – most notably hallucinating an image of their body far larger than it actually is. Many anorexics probably have a weak sense of self and use not eating as a way of trying to be in control in a family where they feel they have none.

On the other hand, new research is offering a different explanation. A team of psychiatrists at the University of Pittsburgh, USA, scanned the brains of anorexic women.

They found that in each case the level of serotonin activity was abnormally high, and linked this to feelings of anxiety and obsessional thinking. The psychiatrists concluded that the anorexics were starving themselves as a means of self-medication, thereby reducing their serotonin levels. They might die of malnutrition, but they would die as calm people.

When Lynn finished school she'd gone on to study medicine at Trinity College, Dublin. In keeping with so many students, during her first year she lived in supervised lodgings in the city. But the following year she expressed a desire to spread her wings a little more. After all, she'd been under the over-watchful eye of her parents for most of her young life. She replied to a small ad placed by students wishing to share their rented house with another. Lynn would have her own, self-contained apartment. Such luxury was unusual at the time and a privilege reserved for the sons and daughters of the wealthy. Lynn had found freedom of a kind.

There are mixed – and indeed conflicting – reports from those who knew her around this time. Some thought her unremarkable in every way. Others recall a bright young woman who had an almost obsessive interest in clothes and personal appearance. Another acquaintance described her as being "nun-like". Whatever the truth about the real Lynn Hutchinson, it seems that her shyness and reserve had not left her. In later life she'd be remembered as gentle and kind: "a quiet lady".

She'd intended to pursue a study in paediatrics but dropped it in favour of psychiatry. Some would say it was inevitable that Lynn should choose this medical specialty.

It's doubtful she'd been able to come to terms with her mother's suicide; by studying psychiatry she'd be in an excellent position to explore her mother's motives. Who knew, but she could perhaps discover an antidote to the poison that was eating away at her own sanity.

She was partially successful. But first would come a breakdown. Whatever brought it on – loneliness, an inability to cope outside the family circle, the pressure of her studies – Lynn fell prey to clinical depression. At her lowest ebb she tried to take her own life, overdosing on pills. She survived, pulled herself together, vowed to avoid stress in the future and took a year out from her studies. Many years would pass before her second attempt, in November 2006. By that time Lynn had escaped the suffocating embrace of her family, thanks largely to a personable young man named Gerard Gibbs.

The two had known each other for some time. They'd grown up in the same district in Tipperary and had met socially on several occasions. The romance came later, when both were in their late teens. It didn't meet with the approval of Lynn's family, however; when she married Gerard there was "a feeling that she'd wed below her".

In fact her husband-to-be was a successful professional in his own right. Although he would not be considered a high-flyer in the general sense of the word, his work was associated with high-flying in the literal sense: he was, and is, a world-class lecturer at the Carlow Institute of Technology, where he offers a Higher Certificate course in avionics, the only study of its kind in Ireland.

Lynn and Gerard prospered. Their combined incomes were considerable and when the children came they decided to move to better surroundings: more secluded, more peaceful. They built the large, redbrick house in Killure, complete with every conceivable feature. The irony was that the working couple only enjoyed their wonderful home at weekends – and often not even then due to pressure of work. They were seldom seen but were talked about, for such is the way in rural Ireland. The family in the big new house were the envy of Killure and beyond.

Despite her loving husband and two bright and talented children, despite her successful career in medicine, Lynn was far from happy. Depression returned to haunt her. The old delusions fostered by her mother and seemingly consigned to the past had, in reality, never really gone away. They slumbered on, even though outwardly Lynn gave little indication of their presence. Gerard noticed them, though. Lynn became obsessed with her appearance, a throwback to her anorexia. She fretted about her weight, pestered her husband about the size of her breasts. Were they too big, too small?

"They're perfect, Lynn. How often do I have to tell you that?"

It grew so bad that she chucked out the bathroom scales, refusing to have another set in the house. She knew she'd be drawn continually to them. Her weight preyed on her mind.

Now Lynn came to believe that her daughter was suffering from the dreaded anorexia. As a psychiatrist at

223

St Vincent's Hospital in Dublin she'd treated a great many girls plagued by anorexia and bulimia. She was convinced she saw the tell-tale symptoms presenting in Ciara. No one else did, Ciara least of all. What began as mild reproaches and expressions of concern were growing into a daily torment for the girl. Her mother simply would not let her be. The family curse had snaked out to encoil a third generation.

Lynn could no longer work. Her depression was interfering with her ability to help her patients. She had swapped her full-time psychiatric practice for locum consultancy at St Luke's General Hospital in Kilkenny. Even that had proved too much to handle; she'd informed the HSE in August that she was taking temporary leave of absence for health reasons.

The delusions were to persist. Worse still, she was suffering from bipolar disorder, known in the past as manic depression, where violent mood swings can cause the sufferer to lose control.

Lynn's delusional depression reached crisis point in the middle of the night of 25–26 November 2006 – possibly sometime around 3.00 a.m. – the time when our internal clock slows our metabolism. Emotionally we're at our most vulnerable, a prey to psychosis. She went into Ciara's bedroom and ordered her out of bed.

That much we know: Lynn confessed to doing this, when she was finally ready to face her questioners. More than two weeks were to elapse before detectives were allowed to interview Dr Lynn Gibbs in St Patrick's Hospital. They found her in no position to offer any rational explanation for her behaviour on that frightful night. The pills she'd overdosed on, coupled with her subconscious horror at what she'd done, had blocked out the terrible memories to a large extent.

Lynn dimly recalled arguing with Ciara. What followed next, however, remains a blur for her. The upshot is that she somehow manhandled her daughter into the en-suite bathroom, forced her head into a bathtub filled with water and drowned her. The State Pathologist, Professor Marie Cassidy, reported seeing only minor bruises on Ciara's body consistent with a struggle. Cause of death: drowning.

The evidence, taken together with Lynn's confession, was conclusive. She had drowned Ciara. The Gardaí had no choice but to charge her with the unlawful killing of her daughter. Only a court could decide whether she was guilty of murder, and if so, the penalty she must pay.

Lynn stood trial in January 2008. Her doctors had given the go-ahead. As was to be expected, the case was something of a sensation. After all, it's not every day a psychiatrist turns the tables and succumbs to the same conditions she treats.

Yet it happens more often than one might think. Research shows an alarming rate of suicide among members of the profession. In most cases, depression lies at the root. Some four per cent of psychiatrists are prone to depression and one per cent experience psychosis. A further three per cent suffer from Obsessive Compulsive Disorder and other mental illnesses.

Psychiatrists sometimes kill too. Australians will remember the case of Jean Eric Gassy, a de-registered psychiatrist who shot his former boss in 2002. It seems likely that he suffered from delusion; he was, for example, convinced he'd contracted AIDS despite there being no evidence of this.

Lynn Gibbs on the other hand gained the sympathy of the general public – as well as those who heard her testimony in court, who listened to mental-health experts who were called upon to testify.

They heard Lynn explain her motives. She believed there was no hope for either her or her daughter. Only death would put an end to their ordeal; the transgenerational curse would be broken.

It is highly unusual that in an Irish court case the prosecution is in agreement with the defence as to the verdict that should be delivered. It's even rarer in a murder trial. Yet this was the situation when the respective legal parties addressed the jury in Lynn Gibbs's trial. Both sides pressed for a verdict of not guilty by reason of insanity.

It was a wonderfully humane plea. And it is to the credit of all concerned that it was proposed and taken up on. For there could be no doubt that in the final analysis Lynn's crime was motivated by love. Her husband Gerard reinforced this when in the witness box.

"She loved Ciara," he said, sobbing.

We can be complacent about this, until we learn that in other jurisdictions they do things differently. For example, in March 2008 a Florida mother was convicted of murdering her seven-year-old daughter in a swimming pool. Amanda Lewis was sentenced to life imprisonment. The sole witness for the prosecution? Amanda's six-year-old son.

"It is long and hard and painful to create life," wrote George Bernard Shaw in 1921. "It is short and easy to steal the life others have made."

The stealing of the life she herself had helped to make was perhaps short work for Lynn Gibbs. Let us hope for mother and daughter's sake that it was. But easy it was not. She was destroying the child she loved, and there is scarcely an act that can break a mother's heart any more than this.

14

SHARON COLLINS
And the Duplicitous Egyptian Hit-Man

You can find anything on the internet. The worldwide web, depending on your experience of it, can be a wonderful blessing or a modern-day curse. It's used by writers – including myself – to research facts, crosscheck data, and to follow leads. All this is possible by means of the search engine, the silent motor that sends its scouts hurtling along the electronic pathways of the net to retrieve information.

Sharon Collins wished to dispose of her partner. She couldn't bring herself to do it so she chose to look for a professional killer.

Had she been doing things the traditional way she'd have followed the well-worn route taken by men and women throughout history. She'd have visited the places which mercenaries – assassins for hire – tend to frequent and wait for business opportunities to come along. She'd have put the word about that a relatively "easy" kill was for the taking.

But Sharon could do none of those things: the underworld was not her world. Instead she settled down in the privacy of her partner's home and switched on her PC to see what she could find.

Sharon keyed in the search term "assassins for hire". She could hardly believe her luck when her search engine pointed her to http://www.hitmanforhire.net. It was exactly what she was looking for.

If you click on that link today you won't find a gun for hire. The FBI and other law-enforcement agencies have ensured that it no longer exists as Sharon found it. Instead you'll find links to embezzlement attorneys, litigation lawyers and the like – all legal and above board.

But go to the Wayback Machine – http://web.archive.org – and key in http://www.hitmanforhire.net. This will invoke a list of pages that no longer exist in their original form; you're looking at archived copies, each one a snapshot of a moment in the life of the internet. The first is dated 16 August 2006; the last is 2 March 2007. Click on any of the links. You'll see the page exactly as Sharon saw it. "*Hit Man For Hire*", it reads – "*The Perfect Solution*".

On the left is a lurid colour illustration of a Hollywood-style gangster, complete with fedora and menacing handgun. A smaller picture of an automatic rifle is accompanied by the following text:

Hitman is the perfect solution for your killing needs. We offer a variety of professional assassination services available worldwide. Whether you are trying to put an end to a domestic dispute or eliminate your business competitors, we have the solution for you.

We are a privately-owned independent enterprise that specializes in reliable contract killings.

We take our business very seriously and are the best at what we do.

Assassinations are the most practical solutions to common problems. Thanks to the internet, ordering a hit has never been easier. We manage a network of freelance assassins, available to kill at a moment's notice. All you have to do is send us an email, along with the details, and wait for further instructions. All the correspondence is done through our secure online forms.

We offer several options to suit the specific needs of our clients.

Each case is analyzed and designed for maximum protection and satisfaction.

Basic contracts start at base cost plus expenses. We require a photograph, bio, and address of the target, along with a deposit. The balance is due no later than 72 hours after the job is done.

You've just read what Sharon Collins would have read on that August day when she visited the website for the first time in search of a paid assassin.

It proved as easy as looking for a plumber. In theory at least.

Sharon had covered her tracks well; she was taking no chances. Submitting false details, she opened a new email account with Yahoo.ie, choosing as her address "lyingeyes98". So far, so good – despite what the Eagles sang in 1975, you *can* hide your lying eyes. On the internet, that is.

The hitman-for-hire website lived up to its promise. Within hours of her sending out the call, Sharon was rewarded with a reply. The name was promising too: Tony Luciano. It had the right ring to it. She'd entered *Sopranos* territory.

Luciano was more than an individual gun for hire, Sharon learned. In his first email he told her he had at his disposal an international band of hit-men, all with formidable reputations, and each ready and waiting to be dispatched to any location in the world – if the price was right.

The price was a hefty $90,000: $15,000 to be paid in advance, the remainder when the sordid business was concluded to the client's satisfaction. It was, of course, to be a cash transaction. Sharon had expected nothing less.

Sharon Coote was born on the outskirts of Ennis, County Clare, in 1963, the youngest of three girls. In her youth she was a normal, fun-loving girl from a respectable family. Absent were any incipient signs of the deceitful, manipulative and coldly calculating individual she would be accused of being.

Upon leaving school she followed a computer course – which would come in handy later on – but didn't pursue a career as such. Instead, aged nineteen, she married her childhood sweetheart, Noel Collins, and settled down in her home-town.

The marriage to Noel lasted eight years and produced two sons, Gary and David, whom Sharon would win custody of. Sharon is devoted to her sons. Throughout her trial they remained by her side at all times.

Between 1990 and 1998, after her marriage ended, she continued to live in the marital home in Ennis. We don't know much about her life during these years. She was on her own, raising her sons. It must have been difficult. But there's little doubt that Sharon, an attractive woman who prided herself on her appearance, was never short of suitors. She was materialistic to the point of fanaticism and, given what would come later, we can speculate that even in those days she was not about to make do with second best. She'd set the bar high: only a rich man would satisfy her.

This need in her, the desire to snare an alpha male with a good deal of disposable income, had been present in Sharon for a long time. Wealthy men impressed her, and in a way it was inevitable that she'd eventually meet PJ Howard – Ennis is, after all, a town of fewer than 25,000 people. In fact their paths did cross briefly when Sharon was nine or ten, a schoolgirl in ankle-socks and pigtails. He was twenty-five and beginning to flex his muscles in the business world.

Patrick James Howard was born in Ennis in 1949. He was an only son who inherited a business – the firm Downes & Howard, a car-sales venture set up by his father together with a friend, Denny Downes. Over the years the company expanded to include property. By the 1990s PJ was a rich man by anyone's standards, with a portfolio of some seventy properties and retail outlets.

At twenty-five he married Teresa Conboy. They had two sons, Robert and Niall, but after eighteen years the marriage ended and they were legally separated. Sharon Collins resembled Teresa in many respects, even down to the blonde hair and outgoing personality. Following the separation she continued to live in the family home, bringing up their sons.

After his marriage break-up in 1992, PJ dated another woman, Bernie Lyons. Tragically she died from cancer in February 1998. It was in November of that year when PJ and Sharon met for the second time. She was thirty-five and the pigtails were a distant memory; she was the proud proprietor of a furniture shop in Ennis. He'd dropped in to browse and was at once captivated by the attractive, outgoing Sharon.

She must have seemed a godsend to PJ, still grieving the loss of one woman and having endured a marriage that had ended in unhappiness. Within weeks of meeting him, Sharon and her young sons had moved into PJ's beautiful lakeshore home, Ballybeg House, a few miles outside Ennis. Besides Ballybeg there was a penthouse in Hotel Las Palmeras on Spain's Costa del Sol, where PJ holidayed as often as his business commitments permitted.

Sharon and her boys had arrived. She'd bagged her alpha male.

PJ also gave her a part-time job as receptionist with the firm. She was not tied to any regular work pattern and could come and go as she pleased. For this she was paid 850 a month with another 1,000 as a "bonus" over and above. At the same time she wasn't without income of her own when she took up with PJ. An entrepreneur in her own right, she was receiving rent from three different properties.

Life for Sharon and PJ, to the casual onlooker at any rate, must have seemed idyllic. They travelled a good deal, staying in the best hotels and leading a charmed existence. But his health was poor. He suffered a severe heart attack in 2000 that necessitated a quadruple bypass. His doctor advised him to slow down; PJ took a back seat in the business, allowing his sons Robert and Niall to take control. He bought a luxury yacht, which he named *Heartbeat* – an amusing reference to his lucky escape. The couple divided their time between Ireland and Spain, increasingly spending longer periods in their holiday home and on the yacht.

Life went blissfully on and the relationship blossomed. But for Sharon there remained a blot on the landscape: she wanted marriage and PJ did not. This was partly due to the fact that his first wife was still alive, and his boys would not take kindly to his marrying a second.

But there was another, more important, reason. Money.

Not that PJ didn't love Sharon – from all accounts he loved her very much – but it seems he did not love her enough to wish to leave his fortune to her. He knew that as his wife, Sharon would be legally entitled to the bulk of his assets upon his death. He wanted his sons, not her, to inherit the business. He felt he owed it to them. By remaining single he would ensure that Sharon had no claim to his estate.

Naturally enough Sharon was far from happy with this arrangement. She had become accustomed to the trappings of the good life and wished to hold onto it.

Fate seemed to lend a hand in February 2003. A tragedy occurred that must surely have made marriage to PJ a very real possibility: Teresa, his first wife, died of a brain haemorrhage.

The pair discussed it at length. PJ suggested that a pre-nuptial agreement would solve the financial predicament – a "pre-nup" is a pre-marriage contract that sets out clearly how assets will be distributed in the event of divorce or death. However, it would not be until the following year, in January 2004, that PJ formally proposed marriage; the two were holidaying in Spain at the time. They could finally make plans. The wedding would take place in Rome a year later.

But Sharon's joy was short-lived. PJ's solicitor threw a spanner in the works: he informed his client that pre-nuptial agreements were not legally binding in Ireland. PJ pulled out. He cancelled the wedding. Sharon was devastated, although she tried hard not to let her hurt show too much.

Sharon was determined, by hook or by crook, to have PJ make an "honest woman" of her. She thought she had found a way. She'd been granted a church annulment of her first marriage and believed that a church-only ceremony might be the answer. But PJ's solicitor thwarted her again. He advised PJ that even a church wedding could leave his assets vulnerable were Sharon and he to separate – or if he died before her. The age difference and his heart condition made the latter a distinct possibility.

In the end an arrangement was reached which Sharon had to accept. In October 2005 in an empty church in Sorrento, they pledged betrothal, but that was as far as PJ was prepared to go. He did, however, agree to be a party to a benign deceit: they'd pretend they'd tied the knot in Italy. On their return to Ireland they announced their "marriage" to family and friends; in November they hosted a lavish wedding reception at Spanish Point, County Clare. Only the couple's solicitors were aware they were not legally married.

We do not know when the idea of getting rid of PJ entered Sharon's head, but it's likely to have taken root sometime in 2005. The failure to secure the pre-nuptial agreement must have been a severe blow. She'd had to settle for a sham marriage, when the real thing would have meant her becoming a very rich woman in the event of PJ's death. His health was not good. He could die at any time. In such an eventuality she'd be left with very little to show from their liaison.

For Sharon Collins was fond of money, of that there is little doubt. Over the years she'd engaged in several "get rich quick" ventures. She ran a successful furniture business, was a fitness instructor to children and was involved in pyramid schemes. But all this was small change compared to the Howard estate. Now, more than ever, she needed to act to secure her future. With this in mind, she began trawling the internet; she was boning up on the intricacies of inheritance rights. Her inquiries seemed to point to a single solution: if she could somehow fix it to look as though she and PJ *had* been married, then perhaps getting rid of him would be worth it.

Over the internet, and without PJ's knowledge, she bought a proxy marriage certificate, a document that appeared to be legal under Mexican law. It cost her $1,295. She arranged for it to be sent to her accountant in Kilrush.

To Sharon's gratification, the accountant was convinced of the certificate's authenticity. Gardaí would later say that this was Sharon Collins's first step towards having PJ and his two sons eliminated. The next step was to see if the fake certificate would pass muster with the Irish authorities.

In February 2006 she put this to the test by applying for a passport under the name Sharon Howard. To her delight, the bogus certificate was waved through. Her application was accepted.

237

Now she was ready to act on her plan.

On 8 August she accessed the website Hitman-for-Hire, and stepped over into the murky world of Essam Ahmed Eid a.k.a. Tony Luciano.

When Sharon Collins made contact, Eid, a fifty-year-old Egyptian, was residing in Las Vegas with two women: his current wife Teresa Engle and ex-wife Lisa Eid. Polygamy seemed to be the only part of the Muslim faith he observed: all told, he'd had seven wives. He would later tell Gardaí, "I have to do it on account of my religion."

His day job was as a poker dealer in a casino. It was not well paid: about $6 per hour. We don't know how seriously Eid took his idea of setting up an agency for assassins. It may well have been simply a ruse to extort money from the gullible. His later actions in County Clare would certainly indicate some such intention. On the other hand he may have been deadly serious, but by and by found himself in too deep. According to FBI records, he bought the domain "hire_hitman@yahoo.com" on 3 June 2006. The website would come many weeks later.

On the other side of the Atlantic, Sharon Collins was opening an email account with Yahoo, using a PC at the Howard's family business in Ennis. The nickname she chose was "lyingeyes98"; the sender was to be "S. Cronin". Whatever the motive on Eid's part, when he received a communication on 8 August from lyingeyes98@yahoo.ie, he acted upon it. Interestingly, the series of emails from Sharon Collins to Eid were sent from an Iridium laptop at Ballybeg

House. The machine belonged to PJ, who was away in Spain at that time. The first, exploratory, email read:

2 male marks in Ireland. Asap. Usually together. Mu like accident. Then possibly a third within 24 hours. Prefera like suicide. Would appreciate a call by return.

She must surely have been delighted when hire_hitman@yahoo.com responded:

I got your email. We will call you within 30 mints . . . can you e-mail us back with more info before we call.

Eid telephoned her as promised. Having spoken to him, she sent a long and fairly detailed email.

Hi.
We were just talking. As you can imagine, I am extremely nervous about sending this message and even talking on the phone.

There are actually three, but two of them would probably be together and the third would not be in Ireland he would be in Spain.

I don't want to give you the names of the people involved just yet, but, I will give you the location and, tell you what I want – ideally.

The first two, live in Ireland, as I said. The town they live in is Ennis, Co. Clare in the west of

239

the country. They are brothers, one aged 27 (big guy) and 23 (not so big). They share a house, at present, but there are two others living in the house as well.

They work in the same place and spend a lot of time together. I do not want it to look like a hit. This is important. I want it to look like an accident – perhaps travelling in a car together or in a boat (they do a lot of boating) off the west coast. Or maybe you have some ideas of your own.

The third is an older man – aged 57 and not very fit or strong. He would probably be in mainland Spain, if not in Ireland. His location would depend on when the job could be done. Again, it is imperative that it does not look like a hit. I would prefer suicide – or is it possible for it to look like natural causes? He's got a lot of health problems.

What I need to know is:

How soon could the above be done? Days, weeks, months? If the job is done in Ireland, is it possible for the second job to be done within 12–24 hours in Spain if that's where he is?

How much would it cost and how much of a deposit would be needded up front? I ask this because, I would have no problem getting my hands on the money immediately afterwards, but it certainly would be very tricky beforehand.

Can it be done in the manner I've stated – without causing suspicion?

Most importantly, if a deposit must be paid – how do I know that you would not disappear with the money and not do the job? After all, who could I complain to?

Where are you located? – Just curious about that.

It might be easier to email back for now. I'm not comfortable talking about it on the phone – even though this phone is unregistered and not used for anything else. I may get a chance to email you again within the next hour, but I will be tied up tomorrow for approx 3 days.

Several emails passed between the two on that fateful day. Tony Luciano assured Lying Eyes that he had "people all over the world in irland and spain too". He told her, "we can do 2 male first and after cool off we will do the third one". Regarding the fee he said, "our price per person is $50000 USD . . . but cause 3 bird in one stone it will be $90,000 USD . . . before we start we have to have a deposit of $45,000 USD . . . you have a choice of fedex money order or cashier check or you can transfer the money to our bank." If Lying Eyes agreed to his terms he could carry out the hits on 19 August.

Sharon did not respond immediately to this mail. She told Tony she'd been away and had no access to a computer, but in her next communication she was very much "on board" with his proposition, even if she did feel a little guilty.

> *I know it must seem terrible of me, but my backs to
> the wall and I don't have much choice. I would
> prefer it if it was just my husband, but because of the
> way he has arranged his affairs, it would be way too
> complicated if his sons were still around and I'd still
> be in much the same situation as I am now.*

She thought his fee was "very fair" but expressed
concern at how she'd get her hands on such a sum: "I
could put my hand on it, in cash immediately, but the two
sons would see it gone and would know it was me and
that would cause too many problems for me." At the
same time she was worried about Tony's suggestion that
there should be a "cooling off period" between the hits on
Robert and Niall and that on PJ. She wrote:

> *How long are you thinking of? I'll tell you the way
> I was thinking. My husband is in spain and lives
> on the top floor of a tall building while he's there.
> If he were to hear that his sons had a fatal accident
> – he might suddenly feel suicidal and just jump off
> the building. Is that too far fetched do you think?*

We don't know what Mr Luciano thought of this idea.
There was a considerable amount of telephone traffic
between the pair during this time: over seventy calls.

He wrote, however, that the murders of Robert and
Niall would be carried out on the nineteenth – by two
women and a man. The plan was that the women would
get close to the brothers and poison them.

He would personally carry out the third hit on PJ, in Spain.

Warming to Eid's idea concerning PJ's sons, Lying Eyes wrote:

They drink in a bar called the Greyhound Bar on the main street in Kilkee. It s easy to find. What do you plan – putting poison in their drinks?

But she had her reservations:

I have to ask you what poison it would be – autopsies would be done and I need to know what they would be concluded from the autopsies. I think it might be easier for your people to stay in a hotel in Kilkee and get talking to them in the bar, but then you know your business – I don't.

Sharon also had questions about the method of disposal of PJ and wished to clarify her own thoughts on the matter:

I would be in Spain with my husband when the above job would be done . . . What would you do about him? Especially with me around. You say you will take care of him yourself. You'd be coming a long way from the US to Spain. I could get the keys of his apartment to you and arrange a time to be out, I would be a suspect, if anything looks suspicious, especially when I would be the one to inherit. Many people think i,m with him for his money anyway – he's a bit older than me etc. and that would also look suspicious.

She ended the email on a rather bitter note:

I appreciate all your help and we will definitely do business. Ive no conscience about my husband, he's a real asshole and makes my life hell, but I do feel bad about the others, however, I thought about it long and hard and I realise that it is necessary or there is no advantage to getting rid of my husband other than not having to look at his miserable face again. But I must be sure that I will be ok financially ect.

S.

This was the first time Lying Eyes had signed herself thus.

The deposit of $45,000 that Tony was demanding was causing a big headache for Sharon. She could plunder PJ's business account, but she knew that such a large withdrawal would be missed immediately by his sons, Robert and Niall. When she shared her worries with Tony, however, he dismissed them with aplomb. He wrote:

This is our business . . . why you worry bout that they don't have the time or days to check about the money cause they will be gone . . . we are planning aug 18 or 19 . . . and your husband aug 20 . . . we can arrange to meet you and get the key or we have our ways in without keys . . .

Tony had also a rather cavalier attitude as to whom exactly he'd be "taking out". He ended the email with this mind-boggling comment: "And we have to have pic of the two guys and your husband too . . . if you don't have it we will figour out that . . ."

Sharon assured Tony that he would definitely get his money. She also added, rather ominously, that she'd probably be putting a bit more work his way in the future. "In addition, there may possibly one more person I might add to the list a little later, but will get this job done first."

It's interesting to speculate on the possible identity of that "one more person" but it was never disclosed. Obviously with the date of her "husband's" demise and that of his sons drawing ever closer and the whiff of all that potential wealth in the air, Sharon was becoming more determined and self-assured. Her goal was within reach. A few weeks down the line she'd be a very rich "widow". She wished to make certain there would be no slip-ups. It was essential that Mr Tony Luciano be in receipt of all the facts regarding PJ's whereabouts in Spain. She went into some detail:

About the boat. I must explain. The boat is not in close proximity to the apartment and when you leave the apartment block, there are lots of shops and vendors all around. They are open until very late and they know him well. I think it would be difficult to get him out without raising suspicion and remember, I need it to look like he has committed suicide after hearing about his sons.

245

Also, the boat is quite big and perhaps, difficult for you to handle, if you are on your own.

I think it is important that I tell you exactly the way it is there. And also point out any complications that might arise. OK?

The apartment is on the top floor of a 14 storey apartment block. It has a private terrace and plunge pool on the roof. An Irish couple, with whom he is very friendly, own the apartment next door. They are in Spain now too, but I think they have tenants in it for the summer – I'm not sure, but I can find out later. This couple also have a boat here, near his boat and if they are not in their apartment, they will be living aboard their boat – another reason why you might find it difficult to get away with taking him out on it.

My husband is planning to go on a boat trip for a few days when I get there – but I don't know when this is or where. I really don't know that until we are going. But I think, wherever it is, when he gets a phonecall about his sons, he will immediately return to his apartment to pack to come home. Unless, he decides to go directly to the airport from the marina. If he does this, then I don't know how you would get him.

I will be there, as you know. How do you suggest we stay in touch, so im not there when you get there. Also I will need to let you know when he gets the news about his sons and what he is doing then.

My husband has a bad heart – maybe when he gets the news about his sons – you wont need to do anything at all (except get your money!), but I feel I should point out all the pit falls to you beforehand. Another complication could be his friends – they might come back to the apartment with us to sympathize with him. The Irish are like that! And there are lots of Irish friends of his out there.

In your experience, when you show up to 'take care of' someone, do they ask you who sent you? Do they offer to pay you to kill that person instead of them? Just wondering . . .

S.

She assured Tony she would send the deposit on Monday, 15 August, by FedEx. She wrote that the $30,000 would be handed to him in Spain; that her husband had a safe in the apartment and that he'd have more than enough cash in it to cover the bill. She offered to give Tony the combination to the safe so that he could help himself, after carrying out the hit. Then she asked if he knew how long the authorities in Spain would wait before releasing PJ's body.

Ill need to get home asap after you ve done your bit to send the rest of the money to you. Will I have to stay there until they release the body or do you think I could leave without causing too much suspicion

247

and let them forward the body to Ireland afterwards?
Perhaps you would know how this works?

By return mail Tony tried to put Sharon's mind at ease. He told her that he operated a professional outfit and that they'd never accept a bribe from the intended target – not even if they offered 10 million. He gave her instructions:

So I want you Monday send the key the pic and the money plus the combinations for the safe and the address for all of them . . . If you have the address for the two guys which is the party add that be great.

Also I want ask you if your husband have a gun or maybe we can used to kill himself or if we not we let him jump from 14th floor . . . I want you stay with him till you leave spain with his body don't leave him it will be suspicious . . . that we recommend . . . I need your phone number in spain too . . . we can contact you there after we done in Ireland . . . we don't call each other by phone maybe is dangerous . . . just e-mail us we reply fast

Thanks

Tony Luciano

The more the pair spoke on the phone and emailed, the more their familiarity grew. Tony called her "sweetie" and told her she had a nice voice. Sharon addressed him

as "Tony" and began signing her emails with her full
Christian name.

In one particularly long email she pours her heart out,
describing how her first marriage was "a disaster", and
how important her two sons are to her. She laments the
fact that PJ

> resents any time I spend with my boys and tried to
> keep me away from them . . . My husband wants
> to control every moment of my life and has a
> dreadful temper. And he make sure I have no
> money of my own. But the main reason im doing
> this is because he is continually trying to force me
> to go out and pick up a stranger for sex. He finds
> the idea of it exciting and insists I must do it or Im
> out and he will make sure that I have absolutely
> nothing. Well I will not do that. No way! . . . He
> never, ever stops pushing for it. Frankly, I don't
> care what he does. I don't care if he has sex with
> hooker or transvestites (of which he is particularly
> fond) everyday, but leave me out of it.

She finishes with:

> Gee, Tony, I must be boring you out of your mind. It's
> the last thing you need to know. Sorry – I do go on.

Between 8 and 15 August there was lots of haggling
between the pair over the money to be paid and the method
of payment. Finally, on the fifteenth, a contract was agreed.

On the same day, Sharon Collins sent 15,000 in cash by FedEx to an address in Las Vegas. She withdrew 13,000 from her own bank account while the remainder was taken from her Credit Union account. She would pay the balance of the deposit, $30,000, to Tony on his arrival in Ireland on 18 August. The outstanding $45,000 would be paid to him seventy-two hours "after the job done . . . this is our contract or you will be the target . . . sorry to say that but this is our policy . . ."

Having FedExed the money to Las Vegas, "lyingeyes98" also sent photos of PJ and his sons via email to "hire_hitman". She wrote:

> *im not sure which photos were which, while I was sending them.*
> *You'll be able to tell which one is my husband . . .*
> *And im the devil in the red dress!*

The photograph showed her sitting on PJ's knee. It had been taken at a Christmas party in Dromoland Castle, County Clare.

Next day, 16 August, Sharon took off to Spain to join PJ. But before leaving she accessed the lyingeyes98@yahoo.ie account and keyed in the tracking number for the package she'd sent to Las Vegas. She was gratified to see it was progressing safely on its way. Tony the hit-man would receive his deposit the following day. At last things could start moving.

At that point the trail of email communications between "lyingeyes98" and "hire_hitman" goes cold. The laptop at Ballybeg House and the Advent desktop computer at Downes & Howard cease to be accessed. But their communication continued: Sharon and Tony were still in touch by phone and email. PJ would testify to the fact that Sharon frequently visited internet cafes while in Spain.

Meanwhile back in Vegas, Tony Luciano a.k.a. Essam Eid was preparing to execute his plan. The timing for the hits was moved back to the end of the month. We cannot say why; there might have been technical difficulties, owing to the fact that Eid was in discussion with third parties. He arranged for his wife, Teresa Engle, to travel to Ireland. She'd be accompanied by a friend, Ashraf Gharbeiah (whom Eid called "Ash"), a part-time police officer. Eid had engaged Ash to "take out" Robert and Niall Howard.

Engle and Ash arrived in Ennis at the end of August. They went to the Downes & Howard offices to inspect the premises with a view to the kill. They were following directions given by Sharon to Tony. Ash had brought with him several narcotics, which would induce a heart attack if mixed with alcohol. The initial plan was to use one or more on PJ's sons. Ash, however, having checked out the firm, decided that the plan was not viable and returned to the US the following day. He would later tell the FBI that he tried to talk Teresa Engle out of continuing with the planned murder.

She travelled on to Spain to reconnoitre PJ's apartment and boat, following instructions from Eid and directions set down in an email by Sharon. She collected a set of keys

251

to PJ's apartment; they'd been left at a specified hotel in an envelope addressed to her.

Back in Las Vegas, Eid was disconcerted to learn that Ash had aborted the hit on Robert and Niall. He would have to travel to Ireland and do it himself. There was a problem, though: he had no visa. It would be a month before his application for one was processed. He'd have to postpone the hit until the end of September.

Or perhaps not. Eid was recalling a correspondence he'd had with a certain Irish soldier . . .

In June 2006 Brian Buckley, twenty-three, was surfing the net. The Dublin soldier was in search of "cheat" codes for a newly released stealth computer game called *Hitman: Blood Money*. He happened upon www.hitmanforhire.net. Not believing for a moment it could be genuine, he clicked on the link that took him to an online application form. He was asked to list his "qualifications" as a potential assassin. He filled it in as a joke, using a pseudonym: Will Buchimer.

He was astonished to receive a reply, on 10 August. It seemed to be bona fide too.

It was, by chance, two days after "lyingeyes98" first made contact with "hire_hitman". Eid had remembered the Irish soldier's application. He seemed ideal for the job: perhaps Eid could get a "local outsourcing" of his hit. He emailed Will Buchimer:

> I have a job for you if you are interested. Two males in Ireland. One in Spain. Asap. Let us know. We will try and call you.

On 28 August, when Eid learned that Ash had abandoned the hit, and that it would be a month before he secured a visa to travel to Ireland to do the dirty deed himself, he began to panic and sent this rather desperate email to Buchimer:

> *Please help us out. I need some strong poison. One of us will be in Shannon. We cannot shift this stuff for security reasons – you know that – so please help us out. Will pay you and I will owe you favourite. Thanks brother. Tony.*

The soldier did not respond to Tony's plea, nor did he respond to his phone calls; he told Tony he had the wrong number, and put the affair from his mind. Eid was on his own. He'd have to finish what he'd started. He'd lost money dispatching Ash to Ireland and needed more from Sharon. He emailed her with the request.

Using PJ's American Express card, Sharon booked two flights for Eid and Engle. Before the pair left the US they made a batch of the lethal poison ricin, with the aid of a recipe Eid found on the internet. They made it from a blend of castor beans, acetone and lye, blended, filtered and dried to produce a white powder, which they stored in a contact-lens case.

Ricin is unusually deadly. Just two granules are sufficient to kill a person – compared to arsenic, which would require about one hundred granules. When Eid and Engle arrived in Ireland on 24 September they were carrying enough ricin to wipe out a small village. But they had just two targets in their sights: Robert and Niall Howard.

The hit-man and his wife booked into the Two Mile Inn hotel in Limerick. Sharon had given Eid instructions that he was to enter the Downes & Howard premises and steal the Advent PC, thereby removing all evidence of their dastardly scheme. He was also to make off with a Toshiba laptop, to have the break-in look like a robbery. She'd left the keys to the office under a brick behind a certain house in Ennis. She'd also given him the code to the alarm so it could be switched off.

Eid and Engle brought the computers back to the hotel. It was at this point that the first of many mistakes were made. Instead of removing the hard drive from the desktop PC and disposing of it – in the nearest river for example – Eid very foolishly dumped the computer in a wooded area at the rear of the hotel. He held onto the Toshiba laptop, however.

It was to figure in his own little plan. He had no intention of doing the job as Sharon wished it done.

Since his arrival in Ireland Eid had been trying to contact Sharon Collins, but Sharon was not responding. This angered him greatly. The woman was costing him time and money.

He was, after all, a soldier of fortune, a freelance doing the bidding of another. Now he decided to do a little freelancing of his own. He was going to pay the

Howard brothers a visit, and make them an offer they'd hardly be likely to refuse.

On the evening of 26 September, at around ten-thirty, Robert Howard answered the telephone. The caller introduced himself as Tony. Word had reached him that Robert had "lost a few computers". He told him he had one of them and would deliver it shortly.

Five minutes later Robert answered his doorbell to find a stranger on the doorstep clutching a Toshiba laptop. He also held copies of photographs showing Robert's father and Sharon Collins.

"I am Tony," the visitor said, handing over the laptop. "I here to say that someone want you dead with your brother and father. They say they pay me one hundred thirty thousand dollars to do hit, but now I change my mind. If you give me the money I won't kill you."

Robert was stunned.

"Wait there," he said.

He snatched the photos from Tony and hurried back into the house to confer with Niall. In the meantime Tony panicked and took off in his hired car. The brothers tried to follow him in their own car, but by then he'd disappeared.

"Who the hell was that?" Niall asked. Robert shook his head.

They notified the police immediately.

The following day Robert received several phone calls from Tony with arrangements for the drop. He issued instructions. Robert would meet two women at a quarter past five in the lavatories of the Queen's Hotel in Ennis. He was to hand over the money. Pay the money and he and his brother would continue living and breathing. It would be as simple as that.

"Simple" was the operative word. Eid was giving the word a whole new meaning. At the specified time, a large Garda surveillance team was lying in wait in and around the hotel. Off the coast of Spain, relaxing on board PJ's yacht *Heartbeat*, Sharon might well have been doing a bit of premature celebrating, believing that "two bird" had gone down "in one stone" with one high-flying bird to be brought down. Whatever she may have been dreaming about, it most certainly bore no resemblance to the fiasco unfolding in the lobby of the Queen's Hotel.

Eid and Engle approached Robert Howard at the bar. They were promptly arrested. Sharon's plan had backfired spectacularly. Life for her would never be quite the same again.

Later that evening Robert and Niall picked Eid out of an identity parade set up by Gardaí. The Egyptian hit-man was charged with extortion, burglary and handling stolen goods, and remanded in custody. His wife Teresa Engle was released without charge – there was only hearsay to connect her with any crime – and she flew back to Las Vegas.

From the outset, Gardaí had suspected that this was more than a straightforward case of a burglary gone wrong. There was no sign of forced entry at the offices of Downes & Howard. Eid had been in possession of both keys and alarm code. Only six people had keys to the building and knew the code: PJ and his two sons, a handyman, a cleaner – and Sharon Collins. Eid also had an inkjet printout of a photo showing PJ and Sharon together. They deduced that there must be some truth to the hit-man's bizarre claims.

The case was unfolding. Detectives could have no inkling at that early stage just how intricate and altogether outlandish the Eid–Collins case would prove to be. It would require two years of Herculean detective work to bring "lyingeyes98" and "hire_hitman" before the courts. Gardaí would conduct over one hundred interviews; analyse eleven computer hard drives; examine countless mobile-phone records; liaise with Interpol and the FBI; and travel to the USA, the UK and Spain. It was an investigation as no other, before or since.

Between September 2006 and February 2007 the plot thickened like Mexican molasses, throwing up some compelling evidence for Gardaí. The FBI informed them they were carrying out their own investigations into Eid and Engle: the pair were under scrutiny for similar extortion activities there. During a search of Eid's Las Vegas home a detective found personal details relating to Sharon Collins.

This vital information put Collins in the frame for the first time. She was arrested on 26 February 2007. At the same time, detectives seized the Iridium laptop she'd been using at Ballybeg House. Sharon had been careful: she'd wiped her "lyingeyes98" email trail. She was not to know that deleted files can be retrieved, even when the hard drive itself has been wiped and reformatted.

These days it's darned difficult to hide your lying eyes.

In the course of their thorough examination of the Iridium laptop, Garda computer experts found more than the Eid–Collins correspondence. They came across a strange email that Sharon had sent to the *Gerry Ryan Show* – a 2FM chat and phone-in radio programme – in April 2006. It had been sent from sharoncollins@eircom.net to grs@rte.ie. She'd requested that her name not be disclosed to listeners. In the message, only some of which could be retrieved, she was complaining about her partner and asking advice.

> *Nothing I do is ever enough. His black moods are unbearable. Tantrums can be thrown at any moment and never in my life have I come across anyone who uses the kind of appalling language that he does. He has a holiday home abroad and likes us to spend as much time there as possible. However, the main attraction for him there is the sex industry. He uses prostitutes and transvestites regularly, but what he really wants is for me to engage in what he describes as 'strange sex'. It's never-ending. He will wake me early in the morning or during the night, asking me when I'm going to do 'something'. What he means is, when am I going to pick up a stranger and have sex with him or when*

will I have a threesome with a male escort and himself. He has even told me he would love it if I would work as a prostitute and that this would really turn him on. I find the idea beyond repulsive. He has insisted on many occasions that we go to swingers' clubs while abroad and has been unbearable to live with afterwards as I do not want to partake in what goes on there. I've witnessed things that I sincerely wish I never had to see. Don't get me wrong, I'm no prude, but I simply do not see myself this way.

The prosecution would later use this email as evidence of a motive to have PJ murdered. But at the time of the fledgling Garda investigation it hardly counted as iron-clad evidence against Sharon.

That was to change when, almost six months into the investigation, a breakthrough came from an unexpected quarter. A porter from the Two Mile Inn hotel came forward to say he had the Advent desktop computer. He'd found it, damp and discarded, at the rear of the hotel back in December and stored it in a boiler room to dry it out.

Through analysis of both computers, the Advent and Iridium, together with two computers belonging to Eid in the USA, the electronic trail of intrigue and deception between "lyingeyes98" and "hire_hitman" was being painstakingly soldered into a strong criminal case.

The mobile-phone evidence recovered was equally damning. Gardaí looked at the phone records for two mobiles, one owned by Sharon Collins, another by "Sharon Howard" as well as two cellphones and a landline in the name of Essam Eid. They tracked around seventy calls made between the sets.

Working on another tip-off from the FBI, detectives searched Eid's remand cell in Limerick prison. There they found a contact-lens case containing traces of ricin. Teresa Engle had admitted, under questioning, to having assisted Eid in making it, and to carrying it into Ireland in September 2006.

When Sharon was arrested she admitted to having used the Iridium laptop at Ballybeg House. She confessed to having keys to Downes & Howard and knowing the alarm code. She also admitted to sending money to a blackmailer with a Las Vegas address. Lastly she told a tale that seemed stranger than her other unlikely tales. It concerned a mysterious novelist. Prosecution would later refer to this story as "the fabulous lie".

Back in September 2006, after Eid had approached Robert and Niall Howard with his unbeatable offer, the brothers had telephoned their father to alert him to the bizarre goings-on. PJ had asked Sharon for clarification. By way of explanation, she told him about a certain Maria Marconi. Sharon said she'd been following a creative-writing course online since 5 December 2005 and that she'd been assigned a successful writer as her tutor.

According to Sharon, Marconi was a bestselling novelist who used a *nom de plume*. What that *nom de plume* was she could not say. Nor did she seem aware of any of the titles of those bestselling novels. Apparently Marconi had encouraged Sharon to write about herself and, as time passed, Sharon found herself pouring her heart out in emails to the mysterious Maria. In April 2006, following a massive row with PJ, her immediate response – having "no other woman to confide in" – was to sit down and tell Maria how much she hated her husband. In her email she attacked PJ "on every level as a man".

Fast-forward to sometime in mid-June 2006 and suddenly Marconi is in Ireland. (Sharon would later elaborate on this amazing tale in a letter to the Director of Public Prosecutions; it was her way of disentangling herself from the cat's cradle of lies and dissembling she stood accused of creating.) She had, she told PJ, allowed Maria to use the Advent computer at the Downes & Howard business premises and also the Iridium laptop at Ballybeg House. She'd also taken the elusive novelist on a scenic tour of County Clare.

She explained to PJ that in July, while they were both in Spain, she'd received an email from Marconi telling her that her laptop had been stolen from Ballybeg. A second email stated that for 100,000 Marconi could have PJ killed, thereby making Sharon "free and rich". Several threatening emails and phone calls had followed from an unknown man. If Sharon didn't pay up, PJ would be sent the incriminating email wherein Sharon had attacked him "on every level as a man". Sharon couldn't allow this to happen, so she paid up. She sent 15,000 by FedEx to an address in Las Vegas. She'd also placed a pair of electronic goggles in the package containing the money; Marconi had apparently left them behind on her trip to Ireland. She was given a tracking number for the package and went off to Spain with PJ, relieved it was all over. Hopefully there'd be no further demands for money.

Astonishingly, PJ believed the story. In May 2007 he financed a ten-day trip to Las Vegas that would allow Sharon to search for Maria Marconi. Once there, she hired a private investigator trading under the deathless name of Venus Lovetere – to try and track down the vanished novelist.

But despite the exhaustive efforts by Sharon, her private eye and Gardaí, no trace was ever found of this Scarlet Pimpernel of the book world. On her supposed visit to County Clare in June 2006 no one but Sharon appeared to have seen Ms Marconi.

Gardaí concluded that she was the invention of a desperate woman seeking to escape the ever-tightening net of suspicion. A hard-nosed criminal would not have been foolish enough to create such a fantasy, they decided. But Sharon was an imaginative woman, and fancied herself as a novelist. Her determination to make Marconi real was expressed in writing to the Director of Public Prosecutions. (In March, April and again in May of 2007 Sharon wrote to the DPP protesting her innocence and outlining how her life and the lives of those close to her would be devastated were a guilty verdict brought in.) In one of the letters she gave an account of taking Marconi to a seaside resort in Clare:

It was summer. I stopped and got ice-cream cones there – a small one for me as I was dieting. I told her how popular the place was. There were quite a few people around on that day. We drove up to the top of the hill and I parked the car in a position that PJ and I often park while we ate the cones.

Sharon told detectives she'd been in regular contact with Marconi, but when pressed could not supply a phone number, an email address or a postal address. Nor was there evidence on her PC of the creative-writing assignments she was supposed to have completed under Maria Marconi's tutelage. During the trial Sharon's defence team could not produce Marconi as a witness.

The trial began on 22 May 2008 and lasted thirty-two days. Ninety-five witnesses took the stand. The trial provided spectacle, gossip and sensation.

It's interesting to note at this point that Sharon was coming face to face for the very first time with Essam Eid. They'd spoken several times on the telephone yet had never met. Their eyes locked across the courtroom. Neither expressed surprise nor recognition.

The prosecution case was a compelling one. Tom O'Connell, senior counsel for the state, summed it up. "Sharon Collins is 'lyingeyes98'," he contended. "She had access to the computer at Ballybeg House and the computer in the office. The only other people with access to those computers were PJ, Robert and Niall Howard, and they were the targets."

He submitted that Sharon had set up lyingeyes98@ yahoo.ie.

"On 16 August, 'lyingeyes98' knew the tracking number and who else knew it? Sharon Collins, because she sent the package. Essam Eid was found in possession of photographs of Sharon Collins and PJ Howard. Sharon Collins admits putting them on a computer. She identified herself as 'the devil in the red dress'. Traces of ricin were found in a contact-lens case in the cell of Essam Eid, in a context where poisoning had been discussed as one of the methods of assassination."

These contentions had been founded, he continued, on several indisputable facts: that Eid had been picked out of an identity parade by Robert and Niall Howard; that Eid himself had admitted to staying at the Two Mile Inn hotel in Limerick. Furthermore, he submitted that the testimonies of Brian Buckley, the soldier who'd accessed his Hitman-for-Hire website, and Eid's wife, Teresa Engle – who'd been granted immunity from prosecution in return for her co-operation with the authorities – would prove conclusive.

Yet despite the overwhelming evidence, Sharon Collins put up a good fight.

In the beginning she appeared calm and in control as she came and went from the Four Courts, flanked by her devoted sons Gary and David.

So confident was she of her innocence that on the twenty-sixth day of the trial she took the perilous step of putting herself in the witness box. With hindsight this proved a foolish move because it showed the jury two very different sides to her character.

On the first day of questioning she came across as self-assured and brazen, smiling at the jury as she rebuffed many of the allegations levelled at her by the prosecution. But the second day saw a dramatic change. Her demeanour was far from confident. The jury now saw a wan, moist-eyed woman buckling under pressure as the questions kept coming.

Counsel referred to the Iridium laptop located in Ballybeg House, the home she shared with PJ Howard. Analysis of internet traffic showed it had been accessed on 15 and 16 August.

"The Iridium wasn't in the house," protested Collins.

"The dial-up connections match exactly," said counsel. "Usage stopped at midnight on the fifteenth of August and began again at eight a.m."

"We couldn't find it," said Collins. "We searched and we couldn't find it."

"There had been contact between 'lyingeyes98' and 'hit_man' at eight nineteen p.m. At eight twenty-six p.m. the user accessed FedEx, with a tracking number. Only you had the tracking number, Ms Collins."

"I gave the tracking number to the blackmailer."

"Was there anyone else at the house that night?"

"I don't even know if *I* was there."

"You are insulting the jury's intelligence," said counsel. "You are telling lies."

"I am *not* telling lies."

"The Iridium laptop is accessed the following morning, the sixteenth of August at eight a.m. or eight ten a.m. and goes into 'lyingeyes98'. Did you notice a blackmailer walking around your house that morning?"

"I didn't set up 'lyingeyes98'. I know nothing about it."

"It's a mantra and you are sticking to it. It is getting very thin in the face of the evidence. At twelve twenty-three p.m. on the sixteenth of August the 'lyingeyes98' email account was accessed on the Advent computer at the Downes & Howard office and straightaway the user carries out a search for FedEx and puts in a tracking number, a number that you as the only person in Ireland knew."

"All I know is I gave the number to a person on the phone," Collins replied. "I definitely wasn't there that morning."

"You went to Spain that same day and suddenly it stops. The mystery person stops, the trail, but we know there was further contact from Spain to Essam Eid's phone."

"I never spoke to a man on the phone. I spoke to a woman."

"Ricin was found in Essam Eid's cell. Can you tell us about how it might have got there?"

"I know nothing about that."

"The hard facts of internet evidence are staring you in the face. Yet you say, 'I know nothing.' You seem to be riding a number of horses."

Collins began to lose her composure at that point, but she rallied through the tears.

"The Marconi experience was the experience I had," she said. "I did stupid things. I did foolish things. I shouldn't have written about PJ, but I certainly did not intend to kill anybody."

"It seems you only tell the truth when it suits you to do so. Your story is growing legs to meet the evidence coming in. You wrote letters to the DPP against the advice of your solicitor. You suggest in one of them that your mother or one of your sons might die if charges are brought against you. This would suggest that you are an emotional and manipulative woman."

"There was a lot of emotion," Sharon countered, "but no manipulation. I'd been hauled out of my home, all kinds of allegations thrown at me. My family were in bits. I was absolutely shattered. I was trying to explain the damage this was doing to me."

"You decided, in the arrogance we've come to expect of you, to write to the DPP, against the advice of your solicitor. You got in here to try and do what you always do, and you sit there trying to manipulate the jury, smiling at the jury."

"I'm not smiling at the jury."

"You were yesterday."

"I'm extremely nervous. When I'm nervous sometimes I smile. I'm here to tell the truth. I've always, always told the truth. I'm not here to mislead anybody."

When asked about the letter she'd sent to the *Gerry Ryan Show*, Sharon admitted she'd written it. She was reluctant to discuss it, however. "To be quite honest with you, I don't want to discuss this at all. I don't see how this relates to murder."

"It shows your hatred of PJ, which could be a possible motive," the prosecutor offered.

"I don't hate PJ."

After a few brief questions from her own counsel, Sharon Collins stepped down from the witness box. She made her way back to where her sons Gary and David were sitting, and sobbed uncontrollably while they comforted her.

Her co-accused, the seven-times-married Egyptian gangster, Essam Eid, didn't take the witness stand. His various interviews with Gardaí were read out to the jury. In the beginning he said he'd had an affair with Sharon Collins, but later retracted this. He denied all knowledge of the emails tonyluciano2001@yahoo.com, the website http://www.hitmanforhire.net, and denied ever having sent emails to lyingeyes98@yahoo.ie. Even when phone records proved conclusively that he'd been ringing Collins from his landline in Las Vegas and his mobile, he replied, "I have no comment . . . I can say I never spoke to this woman at all." When shown an email sent from the laptop at Ballybeg House and asked how a printout of it was discovered at his Las Vegas home, he said he was not responsible for what came into his house. Neither could he explain having Sharon Collins's phone number written in his address book.

His response to Robert Howard having picked him out from an identity parade was, "Is this guy mentally ill? Is he gay?" With regard to the ricin being found in his cell he claimed not to know what ricin was.

"How come I not die?" he asked, if the substance was so lethal.

He seemed to enjoy the celebrity status the trial conferred on him, greeting and smiling at journalists and photographers as he was escorted to and from the court. He had no friends in the public gallery and no one gave evidence in his defence. His wife, Teresa Engle, having shopped him in the witness box, had flown back to the USA soon after. The American authorities had agreed not to prosecute her in exchange for her testimony against Eid, as was the case with Ash, the man who'd turned his back on the contract.

PJ Howard gave approximately two hours of evidence during the trial. The Sharon he spoke of was far from the greedy, scheming woman being presented by the prosecution.

"In the eight years I've known Sharon, she has never asked me for anything," he said. "That's one of the things I find astonishing. I often offered her things and she said, 'No'. If she was given three or four hundred euros for herself, the first thing she would do was make sure her two lads had enough. She'd be far from a greedy person, far from it.

"When I wasn't well she looked after me extremely well. She had a very good life for us. I was very happy with it. I presume she was too. We didn't feel there were any serious problems between us until this situation arose. Prior to that, we were living quite normally."

When asked what he thought of the charges being made against her, he simply stated, "I find it very, very, very hard to believe."

His final day of giving evidence, fifteen days into the trial, was a memorable one. When finished in the witness box he made his way over to Sharon and kissed her. In spite of everything, it was clear that PJ was still on her side. He did not return for the remainder of the trial.

He has since admitted to being angry with Sharon over the allegations she made about his having sex with transvestite prostitutes, but denied her claims.

In the end, though, PJ's loyalty was not enough. After eight weeks of presenting the contents of a nine-volume book of evidence and a jury deliberation lasting eleven hours, Sharon Collins was found guilty on six counts of soliciting a murder, and of conspiracy to murder the three Howards.

Essam Eid was found guilty of demanding 100,000 from Robert Howard to cancel a contract on his life as well as those of his father and brother, and of handling stolen property. But the jury could not decide on three conspiracy-to-murder charges brought against him.

Sharon Collins wept as she was led away. Essam Eid smiled.

In November she was back before the judge for sentencing. Her former husband Noel Collins and PJ Howard took to the stand to plea for leniency. Noel broke down as he related how Sharon was a great mother to their two sons and how her conviction had devastated the family. PJ spoke of her being a caring, loving and decent lady and said he would have no difficulty living with her again.

The judge also heard character testimony from the Bishop of Killaloe, the Mayor of Ennis, Peter Considine and other family friends.

But clinical psychologist Brian Grenville, who examined Sharon Collins in prison, painted a different picture. He stated that the only person Sharon felt sorry for was herself. He said that while she showed concern for her two sons, she became most upset when talking about her own situation. He could not recall her ever displaying concern for the Howards.

"She does not take responsibility for her crimes and so shows no remorse," he said, but concluded that a long prison term could be detrimental to her mental stability.

Before sentence was passed, Robert and Niall Howard made a victim-impact statement.

"We cannot understand how we were propelled from our normal daily lives into such a national drama," one said, "and shudder at the realization that, had the plan been effected, we could have been poisoned to death. We believe it will take a long time, if at all, before we can put the incident behind us."

Sharon received a six-year prison sentence. She plans to appeal it. She's due for release in 2012. Essam Eid likewise received a six-year sentence. In the wake of Sharon's conviction, PJ Howard told *The Sunday Times* that he'd spent nearly 200,000 on private investigators in an attempt to clear her name.

It seems that love is indeed blind.

15

EILEEN MURPHY
The Cliffs of Moher

At the beginning of October 2007 a widower named Keith Lane announced he was stepping down from his voluntary position of suicide watcher. Ever since 2004, when his wife tumbled to her death from Beachy Head on the south coast of England, Keith, a window cleaner, had kept a lonely vigil atop the tall cliffs. He calculated that during those three years he'd prevented no fewer than twenty-nine people from killing themselves by leaping onto the rocks far below.

The irony was that "health and safety" issues had put paid to Keith's selfless work: he steadfastly refused to wear a safety harness when going to somebody's rescue.

Since the 1600s Beachy Head has been a magnet for would-be suicides: there are on average twenty each year. Ireland has nothing comparable, no natural feature from which the desperate fling themselves quite so often. The closest we come are the Cliffs of Moher, that wild and formidable curtain of rock facing the Atlantic off the coast of Clare.

In early 2007, the year in which the "angel" of Beachy Head would take retirement, a young Corkwoman named Eileen Murphy jumped from the Cliffs to her death in the surf boiling at their foot. It was a double tragedy: she leaped with her four-year-old son Evan in her arms.

The Cliffs rank among Ireland's most impressive natural formations. They're tall – about six hundred feet in places – and almost sheer. From out at sea they form a dark, impregnable wall guarding the northwest coast of County Clare. In summer they are spectacular and attract visitors from all over the globe, as well as great colonies of gulls and guillemots that wheel and dive into the surf that crashes incessantly against the rock formations at their base. In January they're a daunting place to be.

The tourbus service from Galway by way of Doolin follows a route that takes it to within a goat's whisker of the Cliffs. In summer most of its passengers disembark here, close to the tourist office. In winter the tourists are few.

The driver had been paying very scant attention to the young woman who'd been sitting in the rear of his coach for most of the journey. She was accompanied by a little boy who looked to be about old enough to start playschool. In fact he'd done that very thing, barely a month before. It was 30 January 2007.

The tour stopped for lunch in Doolin. As the coach entered the vicinity of the Cliffs the driver saw that the

273

woman and child had changed seats. Now they sat near the front. He thought nothing of it.

Some time later the bus pulled into the carpark that overlooks the Cliffs. To the driver's surprise the woman left the bus with undue haste, leading the boy by the hand. He thought she was behaving recklessly.

"I'd watch myself there, missus!" he shouted after her. "It can be dangerous, you know. Especially at this time of year."

His concern was shared by Áine O'Loughlin, a ranger on duty at the Cliffs. The day was a wild one with strong gusts blowing in off the Atlantic and colliding violently with crosswinds from the north and east. It was not a day to go strolling. Nor was it a day to approach the Cliffs with a young child in your arms – and so determinedly too. It was a little boy, Áine saw.

Her concern turned to anxiety when she saw the woman, still carrying the boy, stride past a sign warning visitors not to venture beyond that point. Rangers caution that the pathway she took that day is highly dangerous, skirting as it does the cliff edge. They're continually concerned at the numbers of visitors who choose to venture along that path, despite the warning signs. One ranger remarked that some even went out onto a precarious ledge to take photographs, unaware that it could collapse beneath them. But as it's a right of way there is little anyone can do legally to stop people from taking the path.

Moments after Eileen's departure with her boy, another tourist who'd alighted from the bus at the same time reported that she'd heard a child wailing. The sound seemed to come from the direction of the ocean but she'd seen no one. Áine alerted Tom Doherty, a fellow-ranger.

Tom immediately acted as he had on so many occasions: he went to patrol the cliff edge. He was accustomed to the sheer drop into the foaming waters below. It gave others vertigo. And the cliff walk was treacherous on a winter's day such as this. He scanned the breakers at the base.

At first he saw no sign of the Corkwoman or her boy. But as the swirling breakers receded he caught a glimpse of their bodies close to the base of the cliffs. He alerted the Doolin Lifeboat and other rescue services.

By the time the lifeboat crew arrived at the scene it was obvious that mother and son were dead. The rescuers braved the rocks and surf and succeeded in retrieving the bodies. A helicopter took them to University College Hospital in Galway, where the deaths were officially confirmed. Both had broken their necks in the fall.

The question everyone was asking – as is the case when such a tragedy occurs – was: "What drove Eileen Murphy to do the unthinkable?"

Eileen, twenty-six, had booked into the Skeffington Arms, a small luxury hotel overlooking Eyre Square in the heart of Galway. The hotel receptionist noticed nothing untoward about her. In fact she behaved normally and Evan appeared to be excited about their trip to the Cliffs of Moher the following day.

She checked out of the hotel bright and early and went to the nearby Spar. She wished to buy a ticket for the

O'Neachtain Tours excursion to the cliffs, departing at ten that morning. She was just one of more than thirty would-be sightseers. Yet the curious thing, the sales assistant noted, was that everyone except Eileen enquired as to what time the coach would be returning to Galway.

As the tourbus made its leisurely way through the picturesque villages of Oranmore, Clarenbridge and Kinvara, several passengers observed that Eileen was growing increasingly impatient. While her little son appeared to be captivated by the unfolding panorama of Galway Bay, she herself looked anxious. When the bus made its first stop of the tour at Dungaire Castle the passengers eagerly disembarked to explore the sixteenth-century tower. Eileen was unmoved and remained where she sat.

"How long before we get to the Cliffs?" she enquired of the driver.

She asked it again upon their reaching the Aillwee Cave, a high spot of the trip. By then she could scarcely conceal her impatience.

Only when they'd finished lunch at O'Connor's pub in Doolin did Eileen perk up. She learned that the cliffs were next on the itinerary. Her goal was in sight.

There was no doubting that she'd planned it all. She'd been suffering from depression for a considerable time – ever since she'd separated from her partner.

Eileen's childhood was relatively happy; she was one of three children born to a farming family well respected in that part of West Cork. From all accounts she was a shy girl, and for this reason suffered much bullying at school.

But she seemed to take it in her stride. She was also devout: she was one of the first girls in the district to become an altar server. Her younger siblings Valerie and Liam would follow her example. A local priest who knew them described them as being "very, very shy".

She began work in 2001 in the town of Mallow, as an operative in Kostal, a manufacturer of electrical components for cars, which had opened its plant that year. Soon after, she met and fell in love with Simon Meade, a painter and decorator. They set up home together. They had a son, Evan Jack, in 2003, on whom Simon doted.

But the relationship did not endure. They went their separate ways, Eileen moving back for a time with her parents in Churchtown until 2005, when she was allocated a council house in a new development in Ballyhea, eight miles away. Simon remained in the vicinity and, although separated, the two brought up Evan together.

He was a popular and energetic child, who loved nothing better than playing football and hurling, and following Liverpool, his favourite soccer team. He had learning difficulties, however, and shortly before the tragedy Eileen had enrolled him at the Padre Pio pre-school in Charleville, run by St Joseph's Foundation and catering for children with special needs.

No one knows what it was that deepened Eileen's depression at the beginning of 2007. Some have surmised that the burden of being a single mother and juggling job and home had proven too much for her. On 29 January she decided she could endure it no longer.

She left her car parked outside her home in Ballyhea, packed an overnight bag and together with her boy took the bus to Galway. She left a suicide note on the kitchen table but its contents were never made public. That said, it's unlikely that the note would have explained her motives sufficiently. Suicide notes seldom do.

Furthermore, a young woman will rarely choose to kill herself – and her little boy – as a result of an isolated incident. There is usually a build-up over time: crisis is laid over crisis like unmortared bricks in a wall. It will only be a matter of time before the whole construction comes crashing down; the strain of coping will have become too much for the young woman to bear. She'll have weighed the alternatives before deciding on this, the ultimate course of action. And her depression will have been eroding her self-confidence while increasing her feelings of hopelessness for a long, long time.

On 8 February the then Taoiseach Bertie Ahern officially opened the visitors' centre at the Cliffs of Moher. By that time, extra security fences had been put in place. Nowadays it's a little harder to stray off the beaten track and to find yourself in danger atop the cliffs. There will surely be fewer suicides.

In Clare at least. But on Saturday, 14 July 2007, less than six months after Eileen and her boy perished in the Atlantic, another young Corkwoman drowned herself in another stretch of water, together with another young boy. Thirty-three-year-old Nollaig Owen of Kilworth, a little town to the north of Fermoy, walked into the river Araglin with her son Tadhg, aged nine months. She'd taken the child for a walk in his buggy in early morning, leaving her home on Main Street and heading for the popular walking spot of Glenseskin Wood, through which the little river runs.

She'd strapped the child into the buggy, permitting no escape – even if Tadhg had been capable of saving himself. When they found her corpse it was seen that Nollaig had drowned face down in very shallow water; no other conclusion but suicide could be reached. It emerged that she was suffering from postnatal depression. She'd married a South African but missed being in her home-town, among family and friends. Loneliness had been a contributing factor: she longed to be back in her native Cork. But the loneliness was compounded by problems with her life and relationships. She'd made a suicide attempt four days before the double drowning. Her GP had recommended she be admitted to hospital. Alas, his wise words had gone unheeded.

Nollaig Owen and Eileen Murphy were among several young women in recent years who killed both themselves and their children. In addition to the other cases covered in *More Bloody Women*, in July 2005 Madeleine O'Neill of Carryduff, on the outskirts of Belfast, killed herself and her little daughter Lauren in their home. She was suffering from depression and had indicated she was about to take her own life, but the relevant notes had failed to reach the mental hospital where she was being treated and she'd been allowed to discharge herself prematurely.

We would be deluding ourselves if we thought we will see no more tragedies like that of Eileen and Evan Murphy. A woman bent on suicide will always find a way. It is we as a society that must be vigilant. We must ensure that the more vulnerable among us are listened to when they call for help. More importantly we must be in a position to recognize that call when it's sent out.

Suicide is all too often linked to depression; in fact the two are virtually inseparable. We should therefore monitor very closely those suffering from depression as it is a major risk factor for suicide.

Various bodies throughout the world have compiled lists of the warning signs, things to look for in a person you believe is at risk of self-harming or suicide. It is of course impossible to prevent all suicides; at the same time, several of the tragedies in this book might have been averted had those close to the victims read the warning signs and acted upon them. All things being equal, Eileen and Evan Murphy might well be alive today.

So too might Caitriona Innes and her young daughter Caitlin . . .

16

CAITRIONA INNES
The Letterkenny Tragedy

The location is stunning: beaches skirting the Atlantic to the west, the purple peaks of the Dartry Mountains to the south. So much for natural beauty: those who know Bundoran associate the seaside Donegal town with good times. The hotels, restaurants and pubs are first rate and the craic is good. Like all such holiday towns it attracts visitors the whole year round and so provides employment, whether full time or casual, to a sizable slice of its population, young people in particular. It's a good place in which to grow up.

Greg and Winnie Innes reared six children in Drumacrin Avenue, part of an estate hard by the town centre: four girls and two boys. Caitriona was the second eldest.

On the face of it, there was nothing remarkable about the girl, nothing to set her apart from her scores of friends. In common with many young people attending secondary school in Bundoran she worked during the holidays in several of the hotels and restaurants. Throughout the rest of the year she would find weekend work: for a time in an amusement arcade, later in a bookmaker's shop. She was well-liked and was popular with staff and guests alike.

She fell in love with a youth from the town while working in the luxury Allingham Arms Hotel, named for the nineteenth-century poet, he of "The Fairies" fame.

Caitriona was little more than a child when her boyfriend made her pregnant in 1998. She was seventeen. As so often happens, he broke off the affair on learning of the pregnancy.

She was still living with her parents. Home life was far from stable, however: Greg and Winnie's marriage was on the rocks. Matters came to a head and her father left and went to England.

But Caitriona soon met another young man. She believed this time it was the "real thing". And she was indeed happier. Everyone remarked on it. In May 1999 her child, a girl, was born. She named her Caitlin.

But the second relationship was fraught. Caitriona and her boyfriend did not see eye-to-eye on a great many issues. As a mutual friend said, "They could be seeing each other one week and not speaking at all the next." He was, however, very much in love with her and treated her baby daughter as if she were his own.

Caitriona remained in Bundoran until Caitlin was old enough for school then moved to Letterkenny where she judged – rightly as it turned out – there were better employment opportunities. She also longed for more independence. She found a house to rent and, on the advice of a friend, put herself on a council waiting list for a better one.

Her boyfriend also moved to Letterkenny, found a job and a flat near to where she was living in Whitethorn Close, an older estate near the town centre. In the meantime, Caitriona was settling down and making friends. One was Caroline Gallagher.

A year later Caitriona enrolled at the Letterkenny Institute of Technology for a course of business studies. She could have completed the three-year course and gained a diploma but left the institute after two years, eager to start working. Caitlin was six, doing well and making friends at her school, Scoil Mhuire Gan Smal.

In August 2006 Caitriona began work as a secretary at McNutts, a textile firm in Downings, a town some thirty kilometres from Letterkenny. Life seemed good for the single mother of twenty-five. She was earning a good salary, could afford a childminder for Caitlin, and had found work barely a half-hour's journey from her home. All that was missing was a better house, a real home, and a truly stable relationship with her boyfriend. Their relationship was as rocky as ever.

She could tick off one item on her wishlist when Letterkenny Borough Council allocated her a fine, newly built, three-bedroomed, semi-detached house in Cashel Park. The surroundings were ideal and quite close to where she lived. She could easily keep in touch with friends.

It is here that Caitriona's story becomes vaguer. Although she was a friendly young woman, she kept her love life to herself. We have good reason to believe that around about this time she and the man from Bundoran agreed to go their separate ways. Their on-off relationship seemed off for good. Her colleagues at McNutts noticed that she was quieter at the beginning of May, although her family and friends say that towards the end Caitriona gave every indication of being happy.

The end was unexpected – so shocking that it stunned all who knew the young mother and her charming little daughter. It shook two communities out of their complacency – and forced them to ask searching questions about lives being led in what an American poet once called "quiet desperation".

The weekend in mid-May 2007 began with a flurry of activity. Two happy events occurred almost simultaneously. On the Friday, out of the blue, Caitriona received word about her long-awaited house. The keys were hers to collect after work that day. She spread the good news among her colleagues at McNutts.

The second event was not unexpected. In fact, mother and daughter had been looking forward to it for some time. Caitlin was to make her First Holy Communion that Saturday. She was excited, as was her grandmother in Bundoran, who was all set to make the trip to Letterkenny to celebrate the occasion.

The house in Cashel Park was everything Caitriona could have wished for. She picked up Caitlin at the childminder's and together they walked the short distance to the estate. They were delighted to finally cross the threshold of their new home. Caitlin at once claimed the second-largest bedroom as her own: she was already planning on how she'd decorate it. Caitriona enquired over the phone about arranging a loan to pay for new furniture. She'd planned on moving in the following week.

Caitlin's First Holy Communion day was a huge success. Her grandmother, aunts, uncles and other relatives made the trip from the south-west coast of Donegal to attend the Mass held in St Eunan's Cathedral. The child looked radiant, "like a little angel". The family group later went on to enjoy a celebratory meal in a local restaurant. It was Saturday. The meal over, Winnie Innes announced that she'd arranged a special treat for her granddaughter: a visit to her favourite amusement park in Bundoran. It was to be the happiest day in the child's life. She went with them to the beach, feeling like a queen in her white dress. Her proud grandmother took pictures of her with Caitriona. She went to bed that night in the family home, tired and content.

On Sunday, 13 May, Caitriona and her daughter returned to Letterkenny. They were seen arriving home late in the afternoon.

The following day phone calls were made to the house in Whitethorn Close. They went unanswered. Winnie sent texts to Caitriona's mobile but received no reply. Her office called, as did her best friend Caroline Gallagher.

The phone rang out each time. Messages were left. None was returned. But it was too early for anybody to become concerned.

That was to change the following day, Tuesday, when Caitlin once again missed school. The principal and others at Scoil Mhuire were wondering why the girl hadn't shown up two mornings in succession. Phone calls were made. A local bus-driver noted Caitlin's absence from the school run.

Caroline Gallagher hadn't seen her best friend for days. She went to Caitriona's house, to find the blinds drawn in the middle of the day. Caitriona's car was parked outside. Caroline rang the bell. No answer. She rang again, and again.

Then she did something she desperately wished she hadn't – she looked through the letterbox (as Mary Keegan's sister had done in Firhouse, Dublin). She was met by the horrific sight of Caitriona's lifeless body suspended from the stair-rail.

She'd hanged herself.

Shocked beyond measure, Caroline phoned the police. The Guards forced the door and entered the house. The corpse was cold. The policemen suspected Caitriona had been dead for more than twenty-four hours.

The door to one of the bedrooms was open, its contents and furnishings indicating that it could only belong to a child, a little girl. Lying in bed, wearing a nightdress, her dead face concealed by a duvet, was Caitlin Innes. She'd died within days of her eighth birthday.

The Gardaí quickly ruled out foul play by a third party. There was no sign of forced entry, or indeed anything to betray the presence of another since Sunday afternoon. They could not escape the conclusion that Caitriona had smothered her only child and taken her own life.

The double tragedy moved two communities to tears, "numbed beyond belief". The more because of the mystery surrounding Caitriona's action and her own suicide. The question on everybody's lips was "Why?"

When three days later the two hearses bearing the coffins of mother and daughter made their way through the streets of Bundoran, the town was shrouded in an unaccustomed quiet, broken only by a steady downpour of unseasonable rain. It was 18 May, the start of the summer season. Normally the town would be bustling. But all shops were shuttered, all businesses closed for the day out of respect for the dead. Pupils from Magh Ene College, Caitriona's old school, joined the silent townspeople lining the route to the Church of the Immaculate Conception where the Requiem Mass took place. The tragic pair had been waked the previous night in Winnie Innes's family home, just over the border in Tullaghan, County Leitrim.

The church attendance was great, as clergymen and local politicians came to support the grieving family. Conspicuous by his absence was Greg Innes, Caitriona's father. He'd remained in England while his daughter and granddaughter were being mourned. Moving speeches were made during the service, most notable being that of parish priest Father Ramon Munster.

"Caitriona had everything going for her," he told the congregation. "She was always smiling on the outside, but we never know what is going on underneath."

"We must try our utmost," he continued, "to recognize and help those who live with problems, especially problems of depression."

Did the priest know more than anybody else about Caitriona? There was a general consensus among family, friends and workmates that the young woman was happy. There was no reason to believe she might have been suffering from depression. After all, the previous weekend had brought her double cause to rejoice. There seemed no good reason why she should choose that particular weekend to end her own life and that of the child she doted on.

And yet there were conflicting reports on Caitriona's private life, insofar as she allowed those close to her to peek into it.

"She was a beautiful young woman," said a family friend, "who always put her best side out. But behind the smile she struggled to keep things going because she felt down and depressed a lot."

It seems that Caitriona's far-from-steady relationship with her boyfriend did much to cause – or in any case compound – that depression. A poignant fact emerged soon after the bodies were discovered: she'd tried to call her boyfriend shortly before she hanged herself. It was a "missed call" like no other.

"They were very young when they began going out and Caitriona was really only a child herself when Caitlin was born," the family friend recalls. She had a great liking for the young man who stepped into the gap left by Caitlin's natural father. At the same time she felt that their relationship was always going to be fraught. All too often it's a challenge for a man to accept another man's child as his own. "They had plenty of good times but their relationship was always up and down. I suppose there are thousands of relationships like that up and down the country."

"In fairness to him," she emphasizes, "he loved them both and treated Caitlin like his own daughter. It's just so sad that things have ended this way."

Sean Cannon, the coroner at the inquest, was distressed that Caitriona's suicide was just one more instance in a spate of such tragedies – and that many could well have been prevented. Even though there are numerous suicide support groups each one of us must assume responsibility for those at most risk.

He was alluding to another tragedy that had rocked County Wexford the previous month. Like Caitriona, Adrian Dunne – who was blind – was found hanging in his hallway in Monageer on the outskirts of Enniscorthy. The corpses of his wife and two young daughters were lying in the sitting-room. He'd strangled them all before killing himself. Mrs Dunne hailed from Burt, County Donegal, a little community not far from Letterkenny.

"To tackle this epidemic of suicide and self-harm," Cannon said, "needs all our efforts to prevent the rise of suicide and the grief it causes to family and friends. It behoves us as private citizens to prevent this. We should all look after our mental health and advise other people to do likewise and seek help."

Only later did it come to light that suicide was no stranger to Caitriona's family. There'd been two recent deaths; the first occurred in the second week of April when her uncle, Timmy Heraty, died of a heart attack. He was serving at Finner Camp, the army base in Ballyshannon. The tragedy was compounded when Timmy's older brother John took his own life a fortnight later – and mere weeks before Caitriona's own suicide. It is not too inconceivable that this suicide of a well-loved uncle would have influenced her own.

Suicide, as we have seen, is almost invariably linked to depression. Indeed it's extremely rare for a person *not* suffering from some form of depression to end her own life. Only the non-depressed but mentally unstable fall into this category: in other words, an individual incapable of rational thought. We have no reason to believe that Caitriona was such an individual. Her teachers in the institute at which she studied describe a bright young woman, and certainly not one suffering from depression. If she was depressed, then she concealed it very well.

Yet there are other triggers to suicide. Among them is a sudden change in circumstances. This change need not be negative, although such is usually the case. It can happen that "things get too much" for an individual. That weekend in May was certainly full of changes in Caitriona's life: a new house to look forward to; a First Communion.

Perhaps the biggest change was the split with the man she loved, the parting still fresh after only two weeks.

The last could provide a clue to her motive for suicide. There's also the matter of a suicide note – there was none. This fact may be significant.

Caitlin's Holy Communion would mark a station in both their lives, a very important one. Caitriona was still young enough to recall her own "big day" very well. Could something terrible have happened to her around that time or a little later, something so terrible she'd kept it to herself for nearly twenty years?

Life had therefore changed for mother and daughter. One wonders if the change proved too much for a woman who had for a long time lived with low-level depression, so low-level in fact that no one close to her was even aware of it. She'd joined those people "who lead lives of quiet desperation".

Was Caitriona Innes a criminal? Yes, most assuredly. She killed her only child in what appears to have been a premeditated act. Yet few if any of us will judge her too harshly. She cannot be considered in the same light as, say, Jacqueline Crymble, a woman who took the life of another close to her for reasons of lust and greed. Paul Crymble and little Caitlin Innes were both suffocated to death. But I suspect that Caitriona Innes's motive had its basis in love. I also suspect it was the hardest and most heart-rending decision she made in her short life.

We cannot know what went through her head in those final hours. We can only speculate. I suspect that her mind was made up a long time before. Suicide is seldom the result of a snap decision.

But at the end of the day few would condone Caitriona's act of filicide. She had no right to end the life of a girl whose life had barely begun. She had no right to deny Caitlin a crack of the whip, a turn at the wheel, a ticket in the lottery of life – or any one of the myriad clichés we use to describe chance and opportunity. It's likely that Caitriona wished, as a kind and loving mother, to spare her child pain similar to that she'd herself endured; that she wished to protect her from a hard and pitiless world.

And who's to say that young Caitlin would not have had hard knocks in life? Most of us do. A mother's love, no matter how ardent and unselfish, cannot shield us from all of them. By killing her daughter Caitriona Innes denied her the right to choose, to make her own decisions, for better or for worse. To fall in love, to fall out of love, to love again; to experience loss. To grow to adulthood, to study, to work, to marry and know the blessing of children. Or not. These choices would have been for Caitlin and for Caitlin alone. Instead, another made a choice for her – and thereby denied her any choice at all.

The Letterkenny tragedy, although an isolated incident, was not without its parallels. Twenty-six-year-old Caitriona was not the only young Irish mother in recent years to take the life of her child before killing herself. We've already looked at the case of Sharon Grace, the Wexford mother who in 2005 drowned two of her daughters, and that of Eileen Murphy, who leaped to her death in County Clare, clutching her little boy.

In all likelihood there will be more such tragedies. Whether they're unavoidable is a matter for debate. It's also true to say that we cannot predict them. We can only ensure, each in his or her own way, that the circumstances which can lead to such tragedies are not allowed to come about in the first place.

17

MARY PRENDERGAST
To the Devil a Daughter

Mary Prendergast was released from the psychiatric unit at Cork University Hospital on 10 July 2006. She was forty-six and seemed well. Her depression had lifted somewhat and the prognosis was good. It was the seventh time she'd undergone treatment for her condition.

Two weeks later, however, Mary began hearing a voice. It was female and it came from a most unlikely source: the toilet in her daughter's bathroom. She was at the washbasin one afternoon. It was a rented house, one of a number of identical homes called Glenna Cottages, off Commons Road on the northern outskirts of Cork City. Since losing her husband some years earlier, Mary had lived alone. But on her release from the mental hospital she'd moved in with her daughter Jessica. The arrangement suited both parties: Jessica could keep an eye on her mother; Mary had company and could look after Jessica's little son Jamie, on whom she doted.

Mary was in the bathroom one morning. The house was silent; Jessica and her son were out. She'd just washed her face and pulled the plug on the washbasin when she heard water dripping from the cistern into the toilet bowl. She hadn't noticed the leak before. But there was something odd about the sounds the drip was making. She stopped and listened.

It seemed to be speaking her name.

Mar-y. Drip-drip. Mar-y.

Intrigued, she went closer to the toilet. The sounds were unambiguous now. She could clearly understand what they were telling her.

Mar-y. I-am-Mar-y.

She'd heard voices before. In fact voices, emanating from the oddest of places, had become part of her life. At times they came from the television set; if Mary listened closely she could hear them telling her that the Irish government were conducting a vendetta against her. She was a danger to them. They wanted her dead.

She'd had to be careful. Governments are powerful institutions. They have spies everywhere. They watch their citizens at all moments of the day and night. So Mary gave the government agency no opportunity to assassinate her. She remained in her home, venturing out only when it was strictly necessary. She kept her blinds shut, her doors locked. She knew they were attracted to light, and that lamps could reveal her whereabouts in the house. So she made sure that no lights burned unnecessarily, going from room to room to switch them off. The radio and TV were also instruments by which the government could bug her home; these too she switched off at every opportunity.

Yet the government, powerful though it was, had no control over the water supply. That was her ally. Now in the bathroom, ear cocked at the toilet bowl, Mary understood who it was that was communicating with her through the medium of the water and its incessant dripping.

It was another Mary – a much more potent and spiritual one. It was Mary, the Blessed Virgin, mother of God.

I-am-Mar-y. The voice was more reassuring now. It was warning her of a fresh danger she faced.

You must kill Jessica.

"My daughter?" Mary, not unnaturally, was shocked. Jessica, her only daughter, was twenty-one, a lovely girl and the apple of her eye. Why must Jessica die? What had she done?

You must kill Jessica. Jessica is evil. She is possessed by the Devil.

Mary was horrified by the revelation. The Devil. That was different. The presence of the Evil One in the house was of a higher order than mere government agents plotting her death. If the mother of God was instructing her to drive out the Devil, then who was she to refuse? If driving him out meant sacrificing her only daughter, then so be it.

"When do you want me to do it?"

I will let you know, my love.

And that, for the moment, was that. The drip from the cistern returned to being an ordinary water leak.

Some days later Mary had a strange conversation with her grandson.

"You must kill my mother," the boy told her. "You must kill Jessica."

"What are you saying, Jamie?" She could hardly believe what she was hearing. First Our Lady, now the child. "Why would you want me to kill your mammy?"

"Because she's the Devil!"

So the mother of God had spoken the truth. Not that Mary had doubted it for an instant. Her faith was being tested; that was it. If she doubted the testimony of the dripping cistern, the Virgin Mary was speaking to her again, this time through Jamie. It was truly miraculous. Yet she had to be certain.

"How would you know that, Jamie?"

"Oh, I know all right. She's bad with the Devil. If anyone knows then it's me."

"What do mean, darling?"

"I'll tell you why, Gran. I am Jesus Christ. The Devil and I are old adversaries."

Mary's grandson was barely two years old.

Mental illness and demonic possession have long been considered to be two sides of the same coin. Most believe that possession does not exist at all. In 2006 Christina McKenna and I co-authored *The Dark Sacrament*, a book we subtitled *Exorcism in Modern Ireland*. We'd set out to discover if such a phenomenon existed in our times. We took no sides, simply wishing to present the facts as we found them. We spoke to many Catholic priests and other clergymen, as well as to ordinary people who claimed to be victims of possession and oppression. We concluded that demonic possession – the taking over of a person's identity by a malignant spirit – was a rarity. So rare in fact that only two of the cases we considered could be classified as such. Far and away the greater number of paranormal manifestations were instances of oppression: when entities of one form or another intrude upon the lives of individuals or indeed entire families. They were nevertheless disturbing, whether or not one accepts the existence of such beings or forces.

During our research we were careful not to confuse those cases of oppression with schizophrenia. Indeed we learned from more than one priest that an attempt to exorcise schizophrenia in the belief that dark forces are at work is highly dangerous for the victim, and will of course be ineffective. The opposite holds true also: oppression cannot be treated with psychiatry. The two conditions are by no means interchangeable, even though the symptoms of the one can at times bear a marked resemblance to those of the other.

Science and religion have always differentiated between the two afflictions. Those of a biblical bent will be aware that Scripture also makes this distinction. Matthew, for example, recounts how Jesus went about his healing ministry: "And his fame went throughout all Syria: and they brought unto him all sick people that were taken with divers diseases and torments, and those which were possessed with devils, *and* those which were lunatick." (Matthew 4:24)

Schizophrenia is of itself a comparatively recent diagnosis. It was first documented by a German psychiatrist in 1896. The name was coined by another German, Dr Eugen Bleuler, who brought together the Greek words *schizo*, meaning "splitting" and *phrenia*, "of the mind". Schizophrenics, generally speaking, lose touch with reality and can become delusional. Hearing voices that aren't there may be part of the delusional state.

Yet in 1887, while work on schizophrenia was still in its infancy, a tragedy occurred in rural Galway that was at first thought to be related to demonic possession. It bore some similarity to the sad case of Mary Prendergast. It also led to loss of life.

Poverty is relative. We who live in the island of Ireland in these early years of the twenty-first century imagine we know poverty when we see it. But the poor of our day bear no more than a passing resemblance to the poverty-stricken of Galway in 1887. Mary Rielly was one such unfortunate. When she came to nurse a typhoid patient in Claregalway, a tiny village on the Tuam Road to the north-east of Galway City, her own domestic circumstances weren't much better than her employers', the Dillon family.

The farmhouse comprised two rooms and an adjoining barn. In the latter slept the men: the brothers Thomas and

Michael Dillon, and a farmhand named Peter Flaherty. The women, Thomas's wife Mary and his mother, the widowed Winifred, shared the sole bedroom. And that was all, apart from the small kitchen where the family ate and received visitors. With privacy at a premium it was necessary for Winifred to vacate the bedroom whenever her married son and her daughter-in-law wished to engage in sex. Such were the circumstances that obtained in rural Ireland in those times.

Mary Rielly was a thirty-year-old widow from the city. She had four children, whom she supported by working as a nurse. She enjoyed a good reputation as an expert in the nursing of fever patients, and knew what to do in case of emergency. She came highly recommended.

All went well for a week. While a neighbour looked after her children in the city, Mary spent her days and nights at Michael Dillon's bedside. Truth be told, however, it was no bed in the real sense but a straw mattress spread on the kitchen floor before the fire.

On the evening of 22 April some friends of the family had looked in on Michael, to wish him a speedy recovery and to toast his health. Somebody had brought a bottle of whiskey. Friends and family gathered about the fire and everybody had a glass or two – including Nurse Rielly.

The party broke up long before midnight. Michael's married brother Thomas went to sleep in the barn with the farmhand. His mother and his sister-in-law went to their own sleeping quarters in the room off the kitchen. Mary took up her customary station: a rough couch against the kitchen wall, where she could keep an eye on her patient. She would doze but remain alert to any sounds that might signal an adverse change in his condition. The coal fire continued to burn merrily in the grate.

At three in the morning – the so-called "demonic hour" that I touched on earlier – there was a commotion in the Dillon home. Screams and howls were heard coming from the kitchen. The men heard them clearly in the barn and rushed next door to investigate. Michael's mother and sister-in-law emerged sleepily from the little bedroom. What they saw was inconceivable. It was a sight they'd never forget.

Mary the Typhoid Nurse was dancing wildly about Michael's naked body as he lay face down in the middle of the kitchen floor. He was already dead, and the cause of death was obvious. Even as they watched in horror, Mary, tongs in one hand and whiskey bottle in the other, was heaping blazing coals upon his back. He was singed and blackened, practically from head to toe. Still-burning coals were strewn on the floor about the corpse.

"I burned him!" she screamed. "I done it. I burned the Devil in the place of Michael!"

She smashed the almost depleted whiskey bottle on the floor and turned to the farm labourer.

"Peter, *a stór*," she cried, eyes glazed, "give me a drink and I'll soon have Michael Dillon here instead of the Devil!"

She was arrested for the murder, taken to Galway City and remanded until her case could be examined. It created more than a stir in the county. People were asking what it was that had taken hold of the seemingly ordinary nurse that night.

Was she possessed? On being questioned by the authorities and doctors, she claimed that the Devil had taken Michael's place. Only she could tell the difference. She swore that the only way to secure the safe return of the farmer was to burn the evil entity out of him.

No one believed her. It was too far-fetched, even for the more superstitious of the rural County Galway of the time. Inquiries revealed that Mary had a history of "nervous" problems. It also emerged that alcohol had a deleterious effect on her. She had drunk an unaccustomedly large quantity of whiskey that night and the combined effects of this and her mental illness proved devastating.

She was tried and found guilty of manslaughter, declared criminally insane and incarcerated in the Central Lunatic Asylum for Ireland in Dundrum, Dublin, since renamed the Central Mental Hospital. She remained there until she died in 1922.

Mary Rielly's case was to have an echo of sorts when, in 1895 on a farm near Clonmel, County Tipperary, a woman named Bridget Cleary was burned to death by her husband Michael. He became convinced that his wife had been abducted by "the fairies" and a changeling left in her place.

At first, Michael tried to force-feed his wife with herbs boiled in milk in an attempt to drive out the evil entity. When that didn't work he tried fire. Not once but several times over two days and nights. With the help of others, he dragged her to the hearth and forced her over the burning coals. Her clothes were smouldering, and still the entity refused to leave. He wanted his Bridget back.

As his wife lay moaning from the ordeal, Michael fetched the oil lamp from the table and flung its contents over her. Her clothing caught fire; she screamed. But still she would not die – the changeling stubbornly refused to leave. In the end he dragged Bridget back to the hearth and slowly burned her alive over the open fire. She died in excruciating agony.

He was not declared insane, however. He was found guilty of manslaughter and imprisoned for fifteen years.

More than a century was to pass before the preternatural would be blamed for the taking of another Irish life. This time, however, the Devil and his minions would be shown to be no more than a figment of a diseased imagination. Mary Prendergast's true state of mind would be diagnosed by an expert in his field.

The Blessed Virgin paid her final visit to the house in Glenna Cottages, Blackpool, Cork, on the morning of 29 July 2006. Jessica Prendergast was sound asleep in her bed with her little boy next to her. Down the corridor her mother was roused by an insistent voice in her ear.

Mary, my love!

She sat up in bed and looked at the time; it was five o'clock. She knew without asking to whom the voice belonged.

You can do it now, my love.

Mary was prepared. She'd brought a sharp knife from the kitchen and secreted it beneath her pillow, to await the call she knew would come. She slid the knife out and stole down to her daughter's room.

Jessica was sleeping on her back. The Baby Jesus, also known as Jamie, was lying next to her.

Mary plunged the knife into Jessica's chest.

The young woman woke at once, terrified and in extraordinary pain. Beside her, Jamie opened his eyes. He'd have understood nothing.

Mary, in a frenzy of delusion and religious fervour, brought the blade down again and again. Jessica somehow managed to roll out of the bed and, already fatally wounded, she staggered out to the corridor. Somehow she made it down the stairs.

With the child wailing back in the bedroom, Mary pursued her daughter, hacking at her with the knife. When Jessica collapsed three feet from the hall-door she'd been stabbed forty-four times. The knife had pierced the aorta, the main artery of the human body; that single wound alone would have been sufficient to kill her.

Her mother has no more than a vague recollection of her subsequent actions that morning. We can attempt to reconstruct them, based on the accounts given by others. Some time after the stabbing, while Jessica lay dead close to the front door, she went back upstairs and took little Jamie from the bed. (We can consider it a mercy that the child was too young then for the memory of his mother's slaying to follow him into his subsequent life: it's safe to say he'll remember nothing of those terrible moments.)

Mary put him over her shoulder and carried him down the stairs. She must have been frantic then, because a neighbour reported seeing her running down the street with her precious burden shortly before six. She was heading for the Garda station in Blackpool. Having no transport of her own she went into the office of the Blue Cabs taxi firm and asked for a car to take her to the Guards.

The two men on duty could not help but notice that the distraught woman was no ordinary fare. It was, after all, only six in the morning. The little boy was crying. Mary had blood in her hair, on her forehead, left cheek and left eye. She seemed to be in a state of shock. They alerted the Gardaí.

The officers dispatched to the house in Glenna Cottages found Jessica lying in a pool of blood. The stairs were a mess of bloody footprints; the bed in the main bedroom was saturated.

Back at the station Garda Deirdre Murphy was taking Mary's statement. It was barely coherent. The killer was wailing, shaking, grinding her teeth – displaying all the symptoms of a woman possessed. Her words served only to reinforce this. Mary spoke of her daughter being "bad with the Devil". The Evil One had taken her over, and Jessica was hell-bent on slaying her little boy. The reason? Jesus Christ had somehow entered into Jamie. This the Devil knew and he was determined to destroy the child.

Mary would have to act to avert this catastrophe – a catastrophe that could have dire consequences for the world.

From what Garda Murphy could make out, the woman was determined to save the toddler. Mary was taking her instructions from the Virgin Mary, who informed her that the optimum opportunity had arrived. She need only put Jessica out of action and spirit Jamie out of harm's way.

It was difficult to contact the Prendergast family. Several of them had gone on a fortnight's holiday to a resort in Romania and would not be returning for another three days. But they had one lead: Jessica's brother Wayne, who was still in Cork. The young man arrived at the Garda station greatly perplexed, unable to believe that his mother could be capable of such horror.

Yet he could tell the police that his mother had been behaving very strangely in the days leading up to the tragedy. Nervous and paranoiac at the best of times, she'd visited her dentist for routine work involving the renewal of fillings. But she was convinced that when the dentist injected her gums with anaesthetic he'd actually injected her with the Antichrist.

Was there no end to the conspiracy?

In fact Mary was presenting many of the symptoms associated with paranoid schizophrenia, the most common form of schizophrenia. Patients thus afflicted will experience delusions of persecution – that the government or some other agency is spying on them, reading their very thoughts. They will claim to be on a "mission" from God – or his dark opposite number – that a voice, or voices, instructed them to perform certain actions. While in the ordinary course of things those actions will be benign, they can in a few cases end in grief. David Berkowitz, the infamous Son of Sam, who terrorized New York in 1977 and 1978, was known to frequent cemeteries and swore that voices came from gravestones instructing him to brutally kill certain women.

On the day of Jessica Prendergast's murder, her mother had texted her son Wayne. She was "acting up", he said. She had suffered from her illness for nineteen years yet he could hardly have suspected that her delusion would peak at this time. In all those years she had shown no indications of being a violent person. On the contrary, she'd always been a placid, pleasant woman devoted to her family.

The Gardaí alerted her GP, who came at once. He had her returned to psychiatric care, there to await prosecution. For although it was reasonably clear to all that Mary was a highly disturbed individual, justice would have to be done for the sake of her dead daughter.

The case came to trial in the Central Criminal Court, Dublin, in February 2009. A consultant psychiatrist confirmed that Mary was suffering from paranoid schizophrenia and therefore not responsible for her actions. In accordance with Justice Carney's direction the jury found the defendant not guilty by reason of insanity – a ruling identical to that made in the case of Dr Lynn Gibbs in 2008. Two Irish mothers who'd killed their daughters in the mistaken belief they were protecting them.

Mary was committed to the Central Mental Hospital in Dundrum – the same institution that received Mary Rielly of Galway in 1887. Although more than a century separates the two, it's fair to say that the madness that took hold of them has remained unaltered in the course of those decades.

Could Mary Prendergast's dreadful act have been foreseen? It is all too easy to suppose it could. Yet we are such unpredictable creatures. We do not properly understand schizophrenia, and paranoid schizophrenia even less. We know that those in a delusional state can, like Mary, hear voices that seem real and can come from a variety of sources – or appear to. Medication can suppress such delusions, yet others can quickly take their place. Left to herself, the schizophrenic is capable of great mischief. Nobody, not even she herself, can second-guess her actions.

When under medical care and supervision she will be much less of a danger to herself and others. Yet we cannot lock up all such patients for an indefinite time. To do so would see a return to the Victorian era when the rights of the woman suffering from mental disturbance were severely curtailed. A new generation of pharmaceuticals called "atypical antipsychotics" are very much an improvement on earlier drugs, having as they do fewer side-effects. But drugs will never be the answer. A paranoid schizophrenic can all too easily forget her medication – or decide not to take it at all. In both cases she's putting those close to her (or total strangers) at risk.

So the hunt is ongoing for the rogue gene responsible for the illness. Many researchers suspect that not one but several genes may lie at the root. Its discovery will be the holy grail of psychiatry.

The key appears to be dopamine. Broadly speaking, it's a molecule that acts on the brain in a similar way to, say, adrenaline. It stimulates certain areas, causing changes in mood, thinking and responses to the outside world. Research shows that the schizophrenic suffers from an "overdose" of dopamine. If we can identify the gene or genes that mutate, causing the triggering of too much dopamine, then we are well on the way to a cure. Billions of pounds are being spent on this research. It is only a matter of time before the breakthrough is made.

This is small comfort to the Prendergasts, the Gibbses, the Murphys, and indeed to the many families left bereft by the actions of spouses, siblings and parents. But while we cannot ensure that Ireland will produce no more "bloody women" – those individuals who kill for monetary gain, for revenge, out of motives of self-defence, or because of genuine badness – we can nevertheless prevent good women from behaving irrationally and hurting those they love the most.

There are ample grounds for optimism.